C A N A D A

Niagara Falls, Ontario. The spectacular Horseshoe Falls span 670 metres (2,200 ft) and drop 56 metres (180 ft), attracting over 18 million visitors a year! Niagara derives from the Iroquois language, meaning "thundering noise."

Table of Contents

CANADA

Moraine Lake, Alberta

Elizabeth McIninch
Editor

Foreword

It is a great privilege for me to edit this beautiful volume on Canada as part of the New Millenium Series. The publishers have dedicated themselves to the worthy goal of increasing peaceful relations and understanding between all of the nations and cultures which make up the human family. For Canadians, that goal is entirely understandable. We inhabit a vast, but gentle country, where the accommodation of difference is the raison d'être of our internationally respected national dream.

The Canadian belief in social equality and the common good, the commitment to the principles of moderation, toleration, and inclusion are all part of the constellation of ideas in which this nation has been nourished. Immigrants from all over the globe came to Canada because that constellation cast a light which projected far beyond the gateway to freedom.

This volume has been dedicated to the memory of our late photo editor, Malak Karsh. A Canadian of Armenian descent, Malak believed that the Red Maple Leaf was a symbol to the world community of what can be accomplished through compromise and the celebration of diversity.
Like the great Thomas D'Arcy McGee, one of the Fathers of Confederation, my Irish grandparents dreamed of a new country where justice was as natural as the air and as plentiful as a prairie wheatfield. For them, there was always a special magic in being Canadian. And if you really think about it, for each of us, for all of us-no matter what our ethnic origin or regional attachments-that magic is the same.

Malak, O.C.
Photo Editor: 1915–2001

Halldór Pálsson

Ólafur Gränz

Address from the Directors of
the New Millennium Series

The New Millennium Series is based on our firm conviction that good understanding between peoples of the world of each other's customs and beliefs is of fundamental importance for strengthening cooperation between nations and promoting peace in the world. The intention is to publish a New Millennium Series book for every member nation of the United Nations. The idea has been introduced to over 50 countries and it has been warmly received by everywhere. It is our hope that the New Millennium Series books will form a chain of understanding, tolerance and peace encircling the world. In that chain every country, every book, will be an important link.

The books give carefully selected basic information about each country and its people, presented in a standardized form. The publication is supported by Honorary Council of world renown individuals and has been recognized by the Secretary General of the United Nations. The editors, writers and photographers are all outstanding individuals and well known in the respective country.

To all those who have taken part in the New Millennium Series publications, assisted in many different ways or supported the vision we extend our most sincere thanks.

World Edition Honorary Council together with the National Chairman in Canada

Honorary Council

The Honorary Council consists of well-known and respected members of the International Community who have been recognized for their dedication and unique achievements. The role of the Honorary Council is to bring an added sense of vision to the New Millennium Series as a global catalyst to peaceful relations between nations.

The Honorary Council bears no responsibility for the material in this book or for any aspect of the publication itself.

Canadian National Chairman

In addition to the Honorary Council, each country participating in the New Millennium Series has a National Chairman who is well known for his or her dedication to the well-being of his or her country and the international community at large. The National Chairman advises the publishers, the editor, and the editorial board on the special conditions and characteristics of the designated country under study.

Vigdís Finnbogadóttir
President of Iceland 1980–1996.
Chair, World Edition Honorary Council.

Senator Al Graham
National Chairman,
Canada.

Bertel Haarder
Vice-Chairman, Council of Europe,
Danish Minister of Education 1982–1993.
Council Member, World Edition Honorary.

Nelson Mandela
President of South Africa 1994–1999.
Council Member, World Edition Honorary.

Mary Robinson
President of Ireland 1990–1997,
U.N. High Commissioner
for Human Rights 1997–.
Council Member, World Edition Honorary.

Guy Tozzoli
President, World Trade Centre
Council Member, World Edition Honorary.

**The United Nations
in the new millennium**

Now, as mankind stands at the threshold of a new millennium, the importance of the United Nations is ever clearer. The fiftieth anniversary of the U.N. in 1995 provided the member states with the incentive to tailor the institution to fit the changed times.

Since the cold war ended, the importance of the United Nations has greatly increased and it has been given the opportunity of pursuing its main mission, which is to guarantee world peace and security. The Security Council is stronger than before and the U.N. has widely exerted itself in supporting peace and security, and preventing outbreaks of further violence.

Only through the joint efforts of this international body, of which almost all the world's countries are members, can the poverty and lack of development, the diseases and pollution that are to be found throughout the world, be conquered. These problems do not respect national boundaries, and no single nation alone is able to solve them.

The world's leaders have come together in important meetings and conferences, where they have agreed on policy and plans of operation to redress the most important problems such as human rights, social develop-

ment, the guarantee of food, environmental problems and self-sustaining development.

It is clear that little if any development can take place in countries where the inhabitants are continually threatened and human rights and civil liberties are violated. Peace and security are thus the basis of normal progress and an improved standard of living.

The United Nations is the one institution that has the power to fight for the future of mankind and guarantee coming generations the heritage of an unpolluted natural environment, safe drinking water and unpolluted seas. Today, self-sustaining utilization of the world's natural resources is one of the U.N.'s most important projects.

Throughout the world millions of people are working to carry out the U.N.'s exalted and noble policies, often under difficult and even life-threatening conditions. For all these people it is an encouragement to look back on the last fifty years and to recall the hopes that the founders of the United Nations were counting on in establishing this institution. These ideas and views are still fully valid and will remain a guiding light for the world's inhabitants in the next millennium.

Kofi Annan,
Secretary-General of the United Nations

THIS
IS
CANADA

Peace Tower, Flag and Fireworks.

Welcome to Canada.

Prime Minister's Message.

Canada is truly one of the world's great success stories.

Thanks to the hard work and commitment of generations of Canadians, in our short history of 135 years we have grown from a colony with an agrarian economy to become one of the most advanced and prosperous, industrialized nations in the world. According to the World Bank, Canada is the globe's second wealthiest country per capita. According to the Organization for Economic Cooperation and Development, Canada is number one among modern economies for job creation and economic growth.

Canada is a nation on the cutting edge of the new information economy. Ours is the first country to hook up all our schools and libraries to the Internet. Canada has the longest fibre optic network in the world. And we set bold and ambitious targets that will make Canada a trademark for excellence in e-commerce.

Canada has the world's longest coastline and the world's longest inland waterway. To the North, East and West, Canada is bordered by three oceans that give us the planet's longest coastline and open us to the world. To the South, we have the world's longest undefended border. Our nation covers six time zones and stretches 5,000 kilometres from North to South.

But beyond facts and figures, the true secret of our success lies in our shared spirit of openness, tolerance and mutual respect.

We Canadians trace our ethnic roots to more than 100 different world cultures. There are more than 50 languages spoken by Aboriginal peoples in Canada. The number of visible minorities in Canada has doubled in a decade to more than ten percent of our population. Fully one-third of Canada's children between the ages of five and fifteen are Aboriginal or visible minorities. In Canada's largest city, Toronto, two-thirds of the citizens are neither English nor French in heritage. This gives our national life a truly unique flavour and vitality.

In Canada, we do not ask that you park your heritage at the border when you become a citizen. We welcome the contributions that people from every corner of the globe can make to building our nation.

Canadians are an optimistic and enthusiastic people, who embrace change and are moved by compassion and generosity. Our eyes are always fixed on a new challenge, a larger dream, a better tomorrow. Nourished by generations of doers and dreamers, the Canadian spirit is the key to the history we have lived and the values we embrace. And it is why Canadians share the basic belief that our best days are always still ahead of us.

Bienvenue au Canada –

Message du Premier Ministre du Canada

Le Canada est véritablement l'une des grandes réussites modernes.

Grâce aux efforts et à la détermination des générations successives de Canadiens, en l'espace de 134 ans, la colonie agraire que nous étions est devenue l'une des sociétés industrialisées les plus avancées et les plus prospères au monde. Selon la Banque mondiale, le Canada est le deuxième pays au monde sur le plan de la richesse par habitant. L'Organisation de coopération et de développement économiques classe le Canada en tête parmi les économies modernes aux chapitres de la création d'emplois et de la croissance économique.

Le Canada est à la fine pointe de la nouvelle économie de l'information. Notre pays a été le premier à brancher toutes ses écoles et bibliothèques à l'Internet. Le Canada s'est équipé du plus vaste réseau à fibres optiques au monde. Et nous avons fixé des objectifs audacieux et ambitieux qui feront du Canada un synonyme de l'excellence en cybercommerce.

Le Canada possède la plus longue côte et la plus longue voie navigable intérieure au monde. Borné par trois océans, au nord, à l'est et à l'ouest, il s'ouvre sur le monde entier. La plus longue frontière non militarisée au monde le sépare de son voisin du sud. Notre territoire traverse six fuseaux horaires et s'étend sur 5000 kilomètres du nord au sud.

Mais au-delà des faits et des chiffres, le véritable secret de notre réussite réside dans l'esprit d'ouverture, de tolérance et de respect mutuel que nous partageons.

Les Canadiens sont issus de plus d'une centaine de cultures internationales. Plus d'une cinquantaine de langues autochtones sont parlées au Canada. Les minorités ethniques forment plus de dix pour cent de la population canadienne – une proportion qui a doublé en une décennie. Pas moins d'un tiers des enfants du Canada âgés de cinq à quinze ans sont autochtones ou issus d'une minorité visible. À Toronto, la plus grande ville du Canada, les deux tiers des citoyens ont une ascendance autre que britannique ou française. D'où le cachet et la vitalité incomparables de notre société.

Au Canada, vous n'avez pas à laisser vos traditions à la frontière à votre arrivée. Nous apprécions au contraire la contribution que des gens des quatre coins du monde peuvent apporter à l'édification de notre pays.

Les Canadiens forment un peuple optimiste et enthousiaste qui ne craint pas le changement et se laisse guider par des réflexes de compassion et de générosité. Notre regard est toujours rivé sur un nouveau défi, un plus grand rêve, des lendemains meilleurs. Le caractère canadien, hérité des générations antérieures de bâtisseurs et de rêveurs, est la clé de l'histoire que nous avons vécue et des valeurs que nous épousons. C'est sur lui que repose la conviction profonde que le meilleur reste toujours à venir pour nous.

The Right Honorable Jean Chrétien et Madame Aline Chrétien.

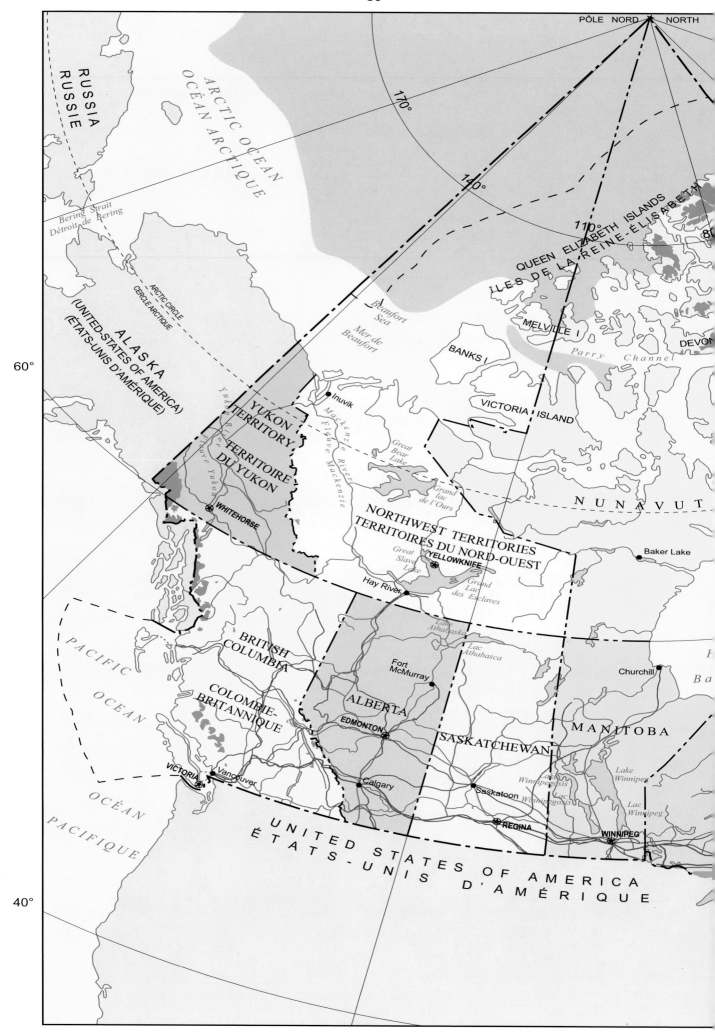

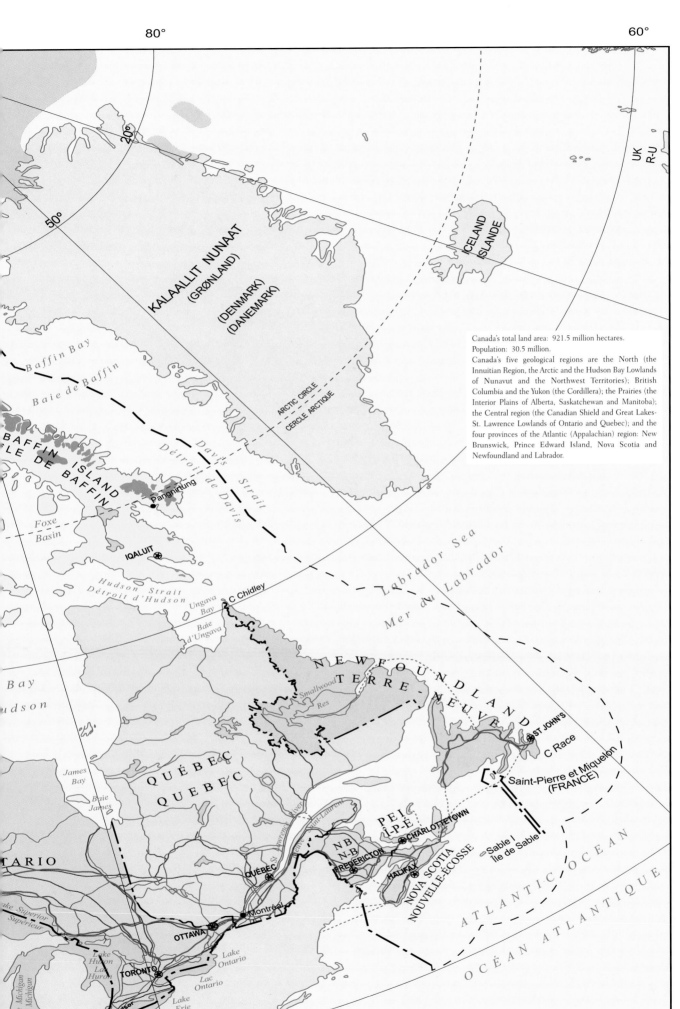

20°

50°

Baffin Bay

Baie de Baffin

KALAALLIT NUNAAT
(GRØNLAND)

(DENMARK)
(DANEMARK)

ICELAND
ISLANDE

UK
R-U

Canada's total land area: 921.5 million hectares.
Population: 30.5 million.
Canada's five geological regions are the North (the Innuitian Region, the Arctic and the Hudson Bay Lowlands of Nunavut and the Northwest Territories); British Columbia and the Yukon (the Cordillera); the Prairies (the Interior Plains of Alberta, Saskatchewan and Manitoba); the Central region (the Canadian Shield and Great Lakes-St. Lawrence Lowlands of Ontario and Quebec); and the four provinces of the Atlantic (Appalachian) region: New Brunswick, Prince Edward Island, Nova Scotia and Newfoundland and Labrador.

BAFFIN ISLAND
ÎLE DE BAFFIN

Détroit de Baffin

Davis Strait
Détroit de Davis

ARCTIC CIRCLE
CERCLE ARCTIQUE

Pangnirtung

Foxe Basin

IQALUIT

Labrador Sea

Mer du Labrador

Hudson Strait
Détroit d'Hudson

Ungava Bay

C Chidley

Baie d'Ungava

N E W F O U N D L A N D
T E R R E - N E U V E

Smallwood Res

ST JOHN'S
C Race

Bay

Hudson

James Bay

Q U É B E C

Q U E B E C

Baie James

Saint-Pierre et Miquelon
(FRANCE)

St. Lawrence River
Fleuve Saint-Laurent

PEI
Î-P-É

CHARLOTTETOWN

Sable I
Île de Sable

NB
N-B

FREDERICTON

QUÉBEC

NOVA SCOTIA
NOUVELLE-ÉCOSSE

HALIFAX

Montréal

A T L A N T I C   O C E A N

ONTARIO

OTTAWA

Lake Superior
Lac Supérieur

Lake Ontario
Lac Ontario

O C É A N   A T L A N T I Q U E

Lake Huron
Lac Huron

TORONTO

Lake Erie
Lac Érié

Windsor

Lake Michigan
Lac Michigan

300	0	300	600	900
km				km

"From the land must come the soul of Canada."
(Canadian historian A.R.M. Lower)

These magnificent photos capture very different faces of Kluane National Park, Yukon Territory, which is an UNESCO World Heritage site.

NATURE

There is no sound in space. The planet beyond the window of the space shuttle is cloaked in mystery, in silent splendor. It is a planet of patterns unlike those ever glimpsed by the human eye. And yet, there is a compelling desire to explore its surface, to discover detail only hinted at from 300 km above.

The perspective of distance brings new meaning to adventure on Earth. It is this gift of reality that enchanted me with the prospect of landing, to awaken my senses to the unique world in which we Earthlings live.

Before flying into the frontier of space, my childhood dream, I felt the excitement of sharing life with others through the medium of photography. My family provided me with the tools for recording and expressing my love of life and nature; my mother, artistic in her poetry and passion, and my father, in his meticulous attention to detail in his photography. The great adventures that I shared in my childhood with my parents and sister encouraged me to explore and photograph the world around me. Filled with curiosity and wonder, I embraced the reality of seeing Earth in the unfathomable black of deep space.

There is much to see on planet Earth. New patterns mean new things to discover. No longer can I take Earth for granted as I might have done before I flew. The patterns unique from space cannot be made of simple systems. Life is complex and nature itself is forever evolving, changing these patterns over time.

The presence of human beings on Earth has been a mixed blessing. On the one hand we rely on nature to protect and nourish our bodies and souls. On the other hand we seem conflicted about the value and immediacy of protecting other life forms from our technical advances. Fortunately, there exist wise men and women who have great vision and the will to protect our natural legacy.

The United Nations has designated many natural areas as UNESCO World Heritage Sites. Other levels of government have protected lands and water in law, such as Canada's national parks. Several of Canada's national parks such as Nahanni National Park Reserve in the Northwest Territories are also UNESCO World Heritage Sites.

One of the few large tracts of land in the world that remains undeveloped is found within Canada, one of the largest political boundaries on Earth. Canada, the land of my birth is surrounded by three oceans; the Atlantic, Pacific and the Arctic. It is home to temperate rain forests, extraordinary mountains including the largest in circumference of any on Earth, glaciers, prairie grasslands, the largest freshwater lakes, the highest tides, fossils, boreal forests, splendid seasons of climate and colour changes, a variety of wildlife and delicate intricate ecosystems that make patterns on top of patterns. Canada is unique to planet Earth.

If flying in space was a dream, then exploring Earth after is a dream with vision and purpose. Communicating joy and passion for our natural world is an heroic way of sharing insight, not just into beauty but into our ability to evolve beyond extravagantly depleting our natural resources. This returns us to the soul of humanity, and the philosophical question of our existence and purpose.

But how will our small steps in spir-

Dr. Roberta Bondar, a neurologist, scientist, and pilot was the first Canadian woman to fly in space aboard the shuttle Discovery in 1992. She holds the NASA Space Medals, is an officer of the Order of Canada, and studied nature photography at the Brooks Institute, California.

itual and humanistic evolution be greeted by our descendents. Through photography we record and express our current understanding and commitment to the natural world. Time will change our techniques for revealing this natural world and it may even change our way of thinking about it. In themselves, photographs are history as we capture light to enlighten and document.

In essence, these historic photographs chronicle both our view of the world, and the world that we view. Whether in a book or in an exhibit, photography is a powerful tool that reflects our insight and vision.

This section on nature contains but a sampling of what Canadians treasure at home in the beginning of this new millenium. It is all part of the natural legacy of Earth.

(*Passionate Vision*, Douglas & McIntyre, Vancouver 2000)

Roberta Bondar writes: "... on a stormy morning, I wanted to photograph the energy of the ocean water in the Gulf of the St. Lawrence as it strikes the shore of the Cape Breton Highlands National Park. These sea stacks, named "Shag Roost" are made of hard volcanic rock, which resists the eroding action of the waves slamming against them."

This charming little fellow posing for the camera of Atlantic Canadian photographer Warren Gordon seems quite at home.

"The clean, sweet earth itself, was garnished with flowers, with vetches crimson, yellow and pink.... They spread in every direction as far as the eye could see." (Mary T.S. Schaffer)

Canada Geese In Flight, Jack Miner's Bird Sanctuary in Kingsville, Lake Erie, Ontario.

When the English poet Rupert Brooke visited Canada in 1913, what impressed him most about this country was its "fresh loneliness." "There is no one else within reach," he wrote. "There never has been anyone; no one else is thinking of the lakes and hills you see before you."

Only 10% of Canada has ever been permanently settled. Nine out of 10 Canadians live in cities and towns that hug the southern border with the United States and vast reaches of the country bear few human footprints. Canada is the second largest nation in the world, topped only by the Russian Federation. It covers nearly 7% of the Earth's surface, but has only half of one percent of its population, a little over 30.5 million.

Like a settling flock of white birds, trilliums dot the forest floor in Springtime at the Bruce Peninsula, Ontario. This joyful scene can be replicated in many other parts of the province, as well as in Eastern Quebec.

Lying 700 kilometres north of the Arctic Circle, Sirmilik (glacier) is one of the richest wildlife areas in Nunavut. Roberta Bondar photographed another feature of its boundless wonders: *"Hoodoos on Bylot Island in Sirmilik National Park are an unusual feature in the Arctic; they require a specific combination of rock type, wind erosion, and dry climate. As I set up for this panoramic photograph, shadows reinforced my concept of blue, white, and brown as the primary winter colours of the Eastern Arctic."*

The white tailed deer Malak has captured as they gaze out thoughtfully into the lens can be seen in open woods, clearings, and cedar swamps. This gracious, animal will appear in your presence before you know it, and then, will flee as quickly and quietly as it came with a flash of its white tail.

Mountain goats – these timid, bearded creatures live in steep, rugged terrain throughout their lifespans in the constant atttempt to avoid predators such as bears, cougars and wolves.

The moose is often referred to as the Monarch of the North – and is a thrilling sight with its antlers measuring about 6 feet (183 cm) from tip to tip.

Canada's national parks comprise more than 350,000 square kilometres of land. Wood Buffalo National Park, which borders Alberta and the Northwest Territories, is our largest national park and the world's second largest. Roughly the size of Switzerland, it is now the only natural nesting site for whooping cranes and is home to an important wood buffalo herd.

Our smallest national park is the St. Lawrence Islands National Park in Ontario, whose 6 square kilometres are scattered across 21 islands and 80 kilometres of the St. Lawrence River. Its unusual inhabitants include the rare black rat snake.

National parks are only one type of protected area. Others include nature reserves, natural monuments and other areas where human activity is limited in some way. Only the United States and Australia have larger areas of protected land.

In Canada, we have protected almost 900,000 square kilometres, an area roughly the size of France and Germany combined. These protected lands make up 9% of our total land mass.

Gros Morne National Park,
Newfoundland.

Of Canada, the legendary Grey Owl once wrote: *"I would like to show you this country with its big waters and black forests and little lonely lakes with a wall of trees all around them, that lie so quiet and never move but just look on and on. You know as you go by them that those trees were there ahead of you and will be there after you are dead."*

Algonquin Park, Ontario, in autumn.

The Call of the Loon

The defining moment of a Canadian vacation at the lake may be the moment one hears the tremolo or wail of the common loon. Now celebrated on Canada's one dollar coin, the loon has four distinct tunes in its musical range.

Canoeing at sunrise.

Owls have often been viewed as symbols of wisdom, perhaps, in part, because of their striking eyes, which can account for between 1% and 5% of their body weight, depending on the species.

The best place to observe snow geese is at Cap Tourmente, thirty miles below Quebec City on the St. Lawrence river. In their spring migration, as they migrate from their nesting areas in the high Arctic tundra, they feed on the plentiful food supply in the nearby marshes. Up to fifty thousand snow geese can appear at the same time in the immediate area of the Cape.

This country is vast, wider than the Atlantic Ocean: 5,514 km from west to east, and 4,634 km from south to north.

St. John's, Newfoundland is closer to Casablanca in Morocco than it is to Victoria, British Columbia. Vancouver is closer to Mexico City than to Halifax, Nova Scotia.

Canada's coastline is the longest in the world and borders three oceans. Straightened out, it would reach two thirds of the way to the moon.

Or, stretched out as a continuous line, it would circle the equator more than six times!

Surrounded by the Arctic, Atlantic, and Pacific Oceans, and home to the Great Lakes, Canada is one of the foremost maritime nations on the planet.

Peggy's Cove on the south shore of the province of Nova Scotia boasts one of the most visited, most photographed still operational lighthouses in the world. This hexagonal shaped concrete tower stares out at the Atlantic from fantastic ancient rock formations.

Canada boasts the world's:

– **longest coastline** (243,792 km) — stretched out as a continuous line, it would circle the equator more than 6 times
– (25% of world's coastline);
– **largest offshore economic zone** (200 nautical miles) — 3.7 million square kilometres, equivalent to 37% of Canada's total landmass;
– **largest freshwater system** — Canada's 2 million lakes and rivers cover 7.6% of our landmass or 755,000 square km;
– **longest inland waterway** (3,700 km) — from the Gulf of St. Lawrence to Lake Superior;
– **largest archipelago** — Canada's Arctic islands, including 6 of the world's 30 largest islands, cover 1.4 million square km;
– **world's greatest tidal range** — 16 metres in the Bay of Fundy. (Fisheries and Oceans, Canada)

Glacier National Park, British Columbia.

Hikers and mountain climbers can climb to the head of the Illecillewaet Glacier on the Great Glacier Trail, or explore caves and mountains in this most spectacular of Canada's National Parks.

According to some theories, what we now call Canada had its origins some 18,000 years ago. For at least 400,000 years before that, most of it was covered by vast glaciers, some up to four kilometres thick.

With the melting of the ice, what would become Canada was gradually revealed. Over time, her spaces became populated by waves of immigrants: Indians, Inuit, Europeans, then peoples from almost every nation on earth. The retreating glaciers left the parent materials for fertile soil. The land was a sea of trees, fish flourished in two million lakes, and the rock itself contained minerals in the five great geological regions of the country.

'The passive corporal bulk of the Shield,' as the poet E.J. Pratt called it, makes up almost half of Canada's total area, while the sedimentary arctic regions, plains and lowlands account for a quarter of the country, and the Appalachians and steep ranges of the Cordillera cover the remaining quarter.

In many ways, these little fellows were responsible for the exploration of much of Canada, as, in the early 1700's, fashionable Europeans demanded felt hats made of beaver pelts. Early explorers and fur trappers spread out across the continent seeking new colonies of beavers as earlier stocks diminished. While beaver dams can be nuisances, causing flooding of roads, railway lines, and the like, beavers are also natural conservationists and, deprived of their activities, forest streams would lose much of their variety and life.

The beaver attained official status as an emblem of Canada in 1975.

The glorious British Columbia Rockies are home to four of Canada's National Parks – Kootenay, Yoho, Glacier and Mount Revelstoke. In this enchanting photo of Mount Revelstoke under moonlight, you can see the wolverine trails intersecting with those of unknown skiers.

Sasagiu on the Grass River.

Mornings are a time of peaceful reflection at Lake Herbert in Banff National Park.

Flying across this country is a "continent's leap," the poet Earle Birney once wrote: we hold "in our morning's hand/the welling and wildness of Canada, the fling of a nation".

The magnificent eagle is found nesting in many parts of Canada but is most abundant on the Pacific coast in British Columbia.

Canada Geese, Two Families. It is very rare to see two families together! The parents of the goslings mate for life and will build their nests near water, the male guarding the female while she is nesting. As these geese have extremely good eyesight and hearing, the male makes an excellent watchkeeper.

Poppa Brown Bear looking for Momma Bear.

The cougar, whose sinewy shape slithers across the pages, is powerful enough to kill a man, although it is normally a solitary and shy animal, shunning human beings.

Mike Beedell is one of Canada's finest adventure photographers.

"Not written on by history, empty as paper / It leans away from the world with songs in its lakes / Older than love, and lost in the miles. . ." (Canadian poet F.R. Scott)

For generations, our minds have been seized by the idea of Canada's North-the lodestone to which the world's compasses point. Our national anthem calls on us to defend "the True North strong and free" and we've even devised an index of nordicity which measures our northness in terms of latitude, climate and human activity.

Arctic Poppies.

In an extraordinary situation near Churchill, Manitoba, a bear and a sled dog become polar pals-playing together, sharing food and curling up with each other on cold windy days. (Mike Beedell)

A herd of muskoxen stoically brace against the wind in Ungava Bay. Their thick coat of wool allows them to survive in this rugged landscape where temperatures can dip to −50C in the winter months. (Mike Beedell)

Polar bears in love.

Little children in an ancient rain forest. Cathedral Grove, British Columbia.

Little girl practicing her craft, Alberta.

Children eating maple taffy in sugar bush in Québec.

Lovely lady Julie from Prince Edward Island.

PEOPLE

Thomas D'Arcy McGee was one of the Fathers of the Canadian Confederation which was created in 1867. He was tragically assassinated only months before his dream became a reality, but through his eloquence, this gifted orator and parliamentarian impacted an entire generation.

His dream was about a new country where justice was as natural as the air and as plentiful as a prairie wheatfield. This was a dream about a country of compassion and compromise; a great experiment in nationhood where people would have freedom to till the soil and toleration to practice their religion.

McGee, an Irishman who had experienced the great tragedies of his homeland, dreamed, as so many of Canada's founders did, of a federation of the heart; a place where unity and diversity could co-exist in harmony.

"I see in the not remote distance," he said in 1860, "one great nationality, bound, like the shield of Achilles, by the blue rim of ocean. I see, within the round of that shield, the peaks of the Western mountains and the crests of the Eastern waves."

In the 1865 debates about Confederation, Henri Joly proposed adopting the rainbow as one of Canada's national symbols: "By the endless variety of its tints the rainbow will give an excellent idea of the diversity of races, religions, sentiments and interests of the different parts of Confederation."

But the notion of welcome to all came much earlier in the nation's history. Long before the coming of Europeans to what would become Canadian soil, the Igloolik Inuit sang in celebration of differences and the fact that 'faces I have not seen before make my house grand!'

The rainbow symbolizes Canada's Unity in Diversity.

Improvised Song of Joy

Ajaia—aia-jaja,,
The lands around my dwelling
Are more beautiful
From the day
When it is given me to see
Faces I have never seen before.

All is more beautiful,
All is more beautiful,
And life is thankfulness.
These guests of mine
Make my house grand,

Ajaja-aja -jaja.

Smiling child of Canada's First Nations.

Undeniably, Canada is an immigrant nation. Search any family tree and our immigrant roots quickly reveal themselves. Our first peoples, the Aboriginals, tell stories of their ancestors arriving on the back of a turtle or by the trickery of the Raven. The French came just after 1600. Yankee and British traders arrived around 1760.

The United Empire Loyalists took up residence after the American Revolution and more Scots came along in the early 1800s, driven off their lands at home. The Irish came to escape the potato famines of the 1840s.

Today, onion domes and minarets shape part of the outline of our cityscapes and the perogies, cabbage tells, cannelloni, bok choy and chow mein of later immigrants have joined the wild rice, maize, tourtière and Yorkshire pudding of earlier settlers on the menus of the land.

About 17% of Canadians today have emigrated from another country. Those born in Europe were most likely to have come before 1971. In the 1960s, changes in immigration policy removed many of the barriers to non-European immigrants. As of 2000, 40% of immigrants to Canada have come from the Asia-Pacific region.

The Asia-Pacific region accounts for as many as 40% of immigrants to Canada.

An Irish Kate from Montréal.

Old Fort Henry Guard and Mascot in Kingston, Ontario.

Glengarry Highland Games in Maxville, Ontario.

Carabana Toronto is the largest Caribbean festival outside the Islands.

*St. Patrick's Day in Montreal, with
Peter Shea leading the festivities.*

The Multicultural Experience

The framework for a multicultural Canada was eloquently envisioned by Sir Wilfrid Laurier, Canadian Prime Minister at the turn of the 20th century, when he boldly proclaimed while beholding an English gothic cathedral: "I would like the marble to remain marble, the granite to remain granite, and the oak to remain oak, and out of these varied elements, I will build a nation that will be the envy of the world."

The very essence of this vision would be echoed nearly three quarters of a century later in 1971 by then Prime Minister Pierre Elliott Trudeau: "A policy of multiculturalism commends itself to the government.... National unity, if it is to mean anything in the deeply personal sense, must be founded on confidence in one's own individual identity; out of this can grow respect for that of others and a willingness to share…"

This ideal underpins the pillars of Canada's multiculturalism: shared identity, social justice and social cohesion. It was designed to integrate, not assimilate, all Canadians in every facet of Canadian life. The policy of multiculturalism has become the unique identifying thumbprint of our Canadian society.

I am part of the Canadian thumbprint. My story as an immigrant began in my country of birth, the Philippines, where to be sick is to be poorer than poor. Indeed, my parents' dream that I become a medical doctor would only be realized with the help of many benefactors at home and in the community. While the days of my youth were not years of amenities, they were, nonetheless, all part of a rich and treasured past. Rich, because the varied experiences I had were to serve as tools to my better understanding and appreciation of the value of human decency – truly, the same overarching value that any country would aspire for her citizens to cherish and uphold. Such experiences would anchor me in Canada in my pursuits as a physician, community volunteer and parliamentarian.

My wife, a dietitian, and I were granted Canadian citizenship in 1974. All four sons – graduates in law, economics, mass communication and business management – are Canadians by birth. The many blessings my family and I have received since first welcomed to Canada in 1968 continue to reach beyond the hopes we first carried with us.

Certainly, it was not within my dream that, twenty years after first landing on her soil and establishing my full-time academic career in pedatric respirology, I would be elected in 1988 to Canada's Parliament and re-elected three times since, putting my medical career on hold.

I am honoured and humbled to be the first Canadian of Filipino origin to attain such parliamentary experience and, later, to serve as Parliamentary Secretary to the Prime Minister and, most recently, to be sworn in to the Privy Council as Secretary of State for Asia-Pacific.

My ministerial portfolio allows me to assist in bringing Canada to the greater attention of the Asia Pacific countries and the region to the attention of Canada, in the realm of foreign relations, trade and investment, and human security and development. Today, this region accounts for 40% of new immigrants landed in Canada.

The Honorable Dr. Rey D. Pagtakhan, P.C., M.P., Minister of Veterans Affairs

Immigration is the underpinning of our shared national experience and continues to mould our national multicultural fabric. Canada's citizens, whether Canadians by birth or by choice, can all take pride in being part of the national vision first conceived by the Fathers of Confederation.

Ours is a nation of diverse peoples united by more than just the glorious maple leaf flag we hail, the respected Canadian passport we hold, and the patriotic O Canada we sing. It is also about the strength of our shared values epitomized in Canada's constitution, declaring our dedication to peace, order and good government. It is about a confident nation and a land of promise that dares to champion peace and prosperity through her story of multiculturalism.

St. Jean Baptiste celebrations in Montreal.

While Canada's multiculturalism is highly visible to the visitor at first instance, there are, in fact, two official languages in Canada, French and English. In Québec, the provincial government maintains an Office de la langue française which enforces the Charte de la langue française. The Charter makes French the official language of the province, and the normal language of the workplace, communications, and business.

Québec is French in origin, North American by virtue of its geographic location, and enriched by a strong, centuries old anglophone presence. While modern Québec is a largely French-speaking society of over 7 million inhabitants (roughly 80% of the population record French as the first language) recent waves of immigration are making it increasingly cosmopolitan. The Québec of the new millennium is a pluralist, modern, dynamic society that is open to the world.

The province is home to about one-quarter of Canada's population. It is the linguistic centre of French Canada but there are people whose mother tongue is French who live in other regions of the country, particularly in Ontario and New Brunswick, which is Canada's only officially bilingual province.

English or French is the mother tongue of most Canadians; that is, the language they first learned in childhood and still understand. Only about 16% of Canada's population speak a non-official language as their mother tongue. Of these, Chinese, Italian, and German are the most prevalent.

Not only are Canada's First Nations rich in culture, they are also linguistically very diverse. The Aboriginal peoples who occupied what is now Canada when the first Europeans arrived spoke more than 50 Indian and Inuit languages and dialects.

But today, at least half of these are either close to extinction (that is, beyond hope of revival) or are endangered. Cree, Inuktitut, and Ojibway, the strongest of Canada's aboriginal languages, still thrive. Each of these languages is the mother tongue of more than 20,000 people.

Robert Tinker's illuminating photo of Banker in Winnipeg.

"MUKLUK" IS INUKTITUT. Most speakers of Canadian English may not realize it, but hurricane, tomato, potato and mukluk are all words from indigenous North American languages. In fact, English is rich with words borrowed from the languages of Aboriginal people. Skunk and raccoon, for example, are Algonquian.

Inuit child with fireweed.

A northern family.

Sikhs in national dress.

Canada Day is always a joyous celebration of a nation's strength through diversity.

Highland lassie in Antigonish, Nova Scotia.

The multicultural face of one of Canada's great cities.

Toronto is arguably the most multi-cultural city in the world. In fact, Toronto has one-twelfth of Canada's population but one-quarter of the country's immigrants. The city's citizens come from 169 countries and speak more than 100 languages. (The top three foreign languages are Chinese, Italian, and Portuguese.) Mass is now celebrated in 35 languages; 200,000 Muslims observe Ramadan; 80,000 Sikhs march in the annual Khalsa Day celebrations; and the city is home to half of the country's Jews. (Mary Vincent, Canadian Geographic)

Certainly, Toronto's growth now rivals that of the Prairies, where, in the early 1900's, immigration led to the same kind of enormous ethnic diversity. In Winnipeg's Elmdale Cemetery, for instance, the names on the headstones of early pioneers are French, English, Polish, Ukrainian, Russian, German, and Lithuanian.

Ukrainian dancing on the Prairies.

A Land of Spectacular Diversity
Where it is mainly the Dream that Counts!

The Governor General, her Excellency the Right Honorable Adrienne Clarkson.

Rideau Hall is the official residence of the Governor General of Canada.

The Filipino community in Canada performing traditional dance.

Her Excellency spoke of the arrival of her family as refugees to Canada upon her swearing in as Governor General: "I believe that my parents, like so many other immigrants, dreamed their children into being as Canadians.

It is customary to talk about how hard immigrants work and how ambitious they are, but those of us who have lived that process know that it is mainly the dream that counts.

I am not talking of fantasy. I am talking of the true dream that is caught in the web of the past as it meets the wind of the future. All of us have this, even if we do not express it. That is what gives a nation, such as ours, its resonance, its depth, and its strength."

German immigrants to Canada, 1911. Close to 10% of Canadians claim German origins.

Thousands of Years of History.

As Peter McFarlane prepared to cross the vastness of Canada in his old Cessna, following the route taken by Europeans in their long procession to the Atlantic, he spoke with aboriginal friends. One, in particular, traced his own ancestry in the Americas back twenty thousand years or more. McFarlane recounts how "the fax rang late at night and a curled-up sheet rolled across the floor. I unfolded it and found a hand-

At the controls over a vast land.

drawn map of Canada. There were no cities or provinces marked; instead the land was broken up into territories of various sizes with largely unfamiliar and

unpronounceable names: Wabanaki, Nitassinan, Kanienke, Tenakìwin, Danaiiwa-ad, Ojibweg, Eeyou Astchee, Kanaisksha-ko, Ktwaxa and Sec-wepemcul'ecw. Across the top Wayne had written "The Old Countries."

When I called him back, he said, "This is what Europeans came to," he said, "ancient civilizations with thousands of years of history."

These Inuit children come from ancient civilizations far pre-dating European exploration.

Student voyageurs following the Alexander Mackenzie route across Canada are seen here on Northern Lake Superior, Ontario.

Hockey, the Great Canadian Metaphor

The excitement and electricity of hockey at an Ottawa Senators game.

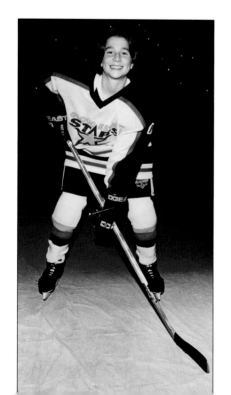

Anna.

One of Canada's greatest runners, Bruce Kidd, once called hockey the great Canadian metaphor. "The rink," he said, "is a symbol of this country's vast stretches of water and wilderness and the player is a symbol of Canadians' collective struggle to civilize such a land."

Hockey is the single most popular sport in Canada. For many Canadian kids, the backyard rink is as much about figure skating and crack-the-whip as it is about learning to stickhandle. For a select few, like young Anna Barrett, it may well be the first step in a journey to the Winter Olympics.

Literature in Canada dates back several millennia to the first inhabitants. A diverse group spread across the top of the continent and speaking many languages, the native peoples included the Boethuks and Micmac of the East Coast, the Six Nations of the Great Lakes region, the Plains peoples, the West Coast tribes, and the Inuit of the Arctic. (Ethnologists at the Museum of Civilization of Canada have documented the cultural heritage of 110 different Native peoples and 10 Inuit regions.) The literature of the first peoples was vast and varied.

Pervading these legends, myths, and stories is a profound belief in an indwelling spirit that is manifested in all things, animate and inanimate, uniting the whole of creation. Most aboriginal literature is oral and cumulative, but original authorship is known in certain cases. The works of two remarkable 19th century Haida poets, the blind poet Ghandl, born in 1851, and the master myth-spinner Skaay, born in 1827, were dictated in 1900 to a young American linguist, John Swanton. These are rich and haunting tales that rival in poetic imagery and narrative power the ancient sagas of the Celts and Nordic peoples.

Canadian literature also includes a vast body of Exploration Literature, beginning primarily in the early eighteenth century, and comprised of the journals and memoirs of the men engaged by the great fur trading companies, the Hudson's Bay and the North West Company. The first great classic was Samuel Hearne's record of his journey on foot from Hudson's Bay to the Arctic Ocean in search of copper in 1770-72. He was guided by a band of Dene people led by their leader Matonabbee. Alexander Mackenzie, the first white man to cross the continent of North America, published his Voyages in 1801. Captain John Franklin described his 1819-22 Arctic expedition in *Narrative of a Journey to the Shores of the Polar Sea*, a tale which is full of the stuff of drama. Franklin's disappearance thirty years later in another Arctic expedition gave rise to numerous plays, poems, and historical accounts of the tragedy.

Canada was established by two founding cultures, French and English, and the literatures in both languages are rich. The first English novel set in Canada was written in 1769 by Frances Brooke, wife of the chaplain to the English garrison in Quebec City. A twenty-three-year-old journalist, Philippe-Ignace-François Aubert de Gaspé, wrote the first French novel in 1837.

Women dominated the early settlement literature leading the twentieth century novelist Margaret Atwood to suggest that Canadian writers had foremothers rather than forefathers. The best known is Susanna Moodie, whose autobiographical sketches, *Roughing it in the Bush* (1852), is a powerful account of the terrible isolation and near starvation conditions of the back wood's farmer. Her sister Catharine Parr Traill wrote pioneering studies of the flora and fauna of Canada, earning the praise of professional botanists. Pauline Johnson (1861-1913), a Mohawk poet, became

Rosemary Sullivan is a distinguished Canadian novelist, poet, and Professor at the University of Toronto.

Canadian Museum of Civilization.

an international star giving public readings throughout Canada, the U.S. and England.

At the turn of the century two remarkable novels were published that grabbed hold of the popular imagination and continue to be read today. Louis Hémon's *Maria Chapdelaine*, published in 1916, is set in the Lac Saint-Jean region of Quebec. It is a classic roman de la terre, or novel- of-the earth promoting fidelity to cultural traditions. Hémon, a Frenchman who had been living in Quebec for less than three years, exactly caught the dilemma of the Habitants or peasant farmers desperate to preserve their language and culture.

In 1908, Lucy Maud Montgomery published her children's classic *Anne of Green Gables*, the story of the quest of a loquacious young orphan for acceptance. Anne and its seven sequels have sold millions of copies in over fifteen languages. The novel has been made into several films, a television series, and a musical staged in Charlottetown, P.E.I. every summer. Green Gables, Montgomery's house in Cavendish (the fictional Avonlea), attracts hundreds of thousands of tourists every year.

In 1945, the Ottawa born Elizabeth Smart published *By Grand Central Station I Sat Down and Wept*, a story of a failed love affair, which has been called one of the half dozen masterpieces of poetic prose in the English language. In 1953, Anne Hébert published her extraordinary

classic *Le tombeau des Rois*. She would go on to win many national and international prizes.

To encourage art in Canada, a Royal Commission on National Development in the Arts was conceived. Reporting in 1951, it recommended government support for radio, television, and the National Film Board, and established the Canada Council for the Arts.

Writing began to flourish. The 1960s saw the establishment of innumerable small publishing houses and literary magazines determined to foster a Canadian literature. One of the finest Canadian novelists, Margaret Laurence, known for her five "Manawaka" novels set in Manitoba, was a byproduct of the current of literary nationalism of the period.

When the Ontario novelist Robertson Davies was asked what he thought he was doing in his powerful Deptford trilogy, which includes the highly regarded *Fifth Business*, he replied that he was trying "to record the bizarre and passionate life of the Canadian people."

Two of the best-known writers to have emerged from the sixties are Alice Munro and Margaret Atwood. Alice Munro, whose international reputation rests on short stories set mostly in Southern Ontario, is credited as one of the founders of the style called Ontario gothic. Atwood is most famous for her dystopian novel *The Handmaid's Tale* and her collection of feminist poems *Power Politics*. She

has won innumerable prizes, including the British Booker Prize, and was awarded France's Chevalier dans l'Ordre des Arts et des Lettres.

French Canadian writing, which includes authors from Quebec, Acadian writers from the Maritimes, Franco-Ontarian and Manitoba writers, also flourished in the 1960s under the pressure of a nationalist movement to preserve French culture. Excellent writers emerged like Gaston Miron, Marie-Claire Blais, Hubert Aquin, Roch Carrier and others. One of the finest novels to come out of Quebec was Anne Hébert's *Kamouraska* based on an actual nineteenth century murder case. It was made into a powerful film by the director Claude Jutra.

Native writers, too, began to come into their own in the late sixties, including Maria Campbell and George Ryga. They would be followed in the 1980s by a powerful resurgence of native novelists and playwrights, including Jovette Marchessault, Thomas King, and Tomson Highway.

Two features of Canadian literature became apparent. 1) It was regional. Each area of Canada from Newfoundland to the West Coast developed a distinctive literary landscape. 2) It was multicultural. The influx of immigrant writers to Canada from all parts of the world in the sixties and seventies enriched English and French literature.

One of the most famous among them, Michael Ondaatje, internationally acclaimed author of *The English Patient,* arrived in Canada at the age of nineteen. Grafting the new culture onto old roots proved fascinating, as is evident in the work of writers like Rohinton Mistry, originally from India, Josef Skvorecky who arrived as a political refugee from Czechoslovakia, and Dany Lafeffière from Haiti.

In 1953, the Stratford Festival, in Stratford Ontario, opened with Alec Guinness in Richard III, directed by Tyrone Guthrie. Though specializing in Shakespeare, Stratford also mounts other plays from classical Greek to modern. The town attracts hundreds of thousands of visitors during the festival season from May to November.

The festival has evolved to include concerts, operas, a Fringe Festival and even an Academy featuring seminars on theatre design, costumes, and acting. The rival Shaw Festival was

The Festival Theatre, Stratford.

The meticulously restored Winter Garden Theatre, Toronto. Patrons are meant to feel they have walked into a rooftop garden that is in bloom year round! (Ontario Heritage Foundation)

founded in 1962 in Niagara-On-The-Lake. Focused mainly on the works of Bernard Shaw, it also includes other playwrights from Ibsen to Pinter.

The 1960s saw the opening of regional theatres across Canada from the Neptune Theatre in Halifax to the Vancouver Playhouse. Internationally renowned playwrights like Michel Tremblay and George Walker wrote wonderfully lively, in some cases comic and darkly violent plays about working class life in Montréal and Toronto respectively.

The Museum of Civilization in the capital city, Ottawa, is the premier place to view some of the magnificent art of the indigenous peoples of Canada, from huge housepoles, masks, and ceremonial artifacts, to the work of contemporary sculptors like the great Haida carver, Bill Reid.

The Group of Seven have been credited with establishing a Canadian art. Beginning in the 1910s, they trekked into the wilderness with their easels in backpacks. Most famous are Tom Thomson and Lawren Harris whose harsh, lonely landscapes of the Canadian Shield express the spirit presence in the landscape. On the West Coast, the visionary painter Emily Carr travelled alone by canoe to the Queen Charlotte Islands. In Quebec in 1947, the abstract artist Paul-Emile Borduas published the manifesto *Refus Global* and started a

revolutionary art movement that produced painters like Jean Paul Riopelle. Others like Jean Paul Lemieux painted emblematic landscapes of rural Quebec that capture the complexity of Quebec culture.

Painting also followed regional developments, from the Maritime artists like Alex Colville and Christopher and Mary Pratt who gave realism a distinctly Canadian spin, to the Canadian-born Ukrainian artist William Kurelek who recorded the austere emptiness and monumental grandeur of the prairies. In Toronto, the tireless pun artist, Charles Pachter, was deconstructing Canadian iconography in his paintings, that included Queen Elizabeth II on a Moose. Postmodernism has flourished in the work of artists like Betty Goodwin, Vera Frenkel, and John Scott.

The classical musical tradition in Canada is rich in performers like Glenn Gould, long considered the world's greatest interpreter of Bach; the opera singers, Teresa Stratas and Maureen Forrester, and most recently, Ben Heppner. Composers include R. Murray Schafer and Christos Hatzis. Popular musicians have achieved international fame like the jazz pianist Oscar Peterson, the Celtic singer Loreena McKennitt, the Scottish fiddler Natalie MacMaster, and folk singers Leonard Cohen, Joni Mitchell, and Neil Young. Contemporary pop

singers include Celine Dion, Sarah McLaughlin, Brian Adams, and K.D. Lang, as well as groups like Blue Rodeo, Bare Naked Ladies, Rush – and Crash Test Dummies.

In spite of the proximity and pressures of the American film industry, an independent film industry has emerged under the creative leadership of directors like the gifted David Cronenberg, Patricia Rozema, and Atom Egoyen, and from Quebec, Denys Arcand, Claude Jutra, and Michel Brault.

An amusing footnote is that many film stars thought to be American, like Mary Pickford, Donald Sutherland, Christopher Plummer, and Star Trek's own William Shatner, Keanu Reeves, Kiefer Sutherland and Jim Carrey, are actually Canadian!

Royal Winnipeg Ballet.

A Special Magic

Champlain gazes over the St. Lawrence river, gateway to a continent.

"You could hardly hope to find a more beautiful country," wrote the founder of New France, the brilliant cartographer and explorer, Samuel de Champlain, as he sailed up the St. Lawrence for the first time. In 1608, he would bring settlers to stay at the Habitation of Québec, the oldest permanent settlement in North America.

HISTORY

Editor's Note: It is said that the history of Canada is a whole process of discovery; a spirit of continuing adventure which the country was, is, and always will be. This section is designed to open some windows on that process. As the book progresses, the reader will gain more insight into our 'mysterious attic' as Peter C. Newmann put it so well, in the chapters on our provinces and territories. It is my hope that you will find something in the tales that are told that will encourage you to go off and discover more for yourself.

Someone once said that Canada is an unfinished struggle. That may be true, but the centuries long sowing of the seeds of the Canadian identity is, even more importantly, just a great story! Indeed, that story is a fascinating exercise in how a gutsy, resilient and purposeful people defied all the odds, building and imagining a beautiful country with purpose and conviction.

One must think back well before the period of responsible government and the epic age of Confederation to the daring individuals who set out to explore a continent. Some wrote about its unimaginable potential and endless geographical expanses, captivating readers of their time.

The accounts of the mid 18th century voyages of the Englishman, Samuel Hearne in the company of the wise, fierce and courageous Dene native, Matonnabbee – which made them the first expedition to reach the Arctic overland – were read in French, German and Dutch translations as well as two editions in English.

This great chapter in Canadian exploration writing was not just about the hardships, the challenge, and the splendor of early northern voyages. It was about the bonds between aboriginal and European adventurers; a meeting of minds between unique cultures and ancient inheritances. The friendship between Hearne and Matonnabbee, formed in a frontier which knew no end, was to become a vital symbol in the nascent understanding of what Canada could become and what it was meant to be.

Decades later, the extraordinary partnership of Robert Baldwin and Louis Hippolyte LaFontaine culminated in an historic Reform alliance in the House of Assembly of a United Canada, which had been created in 1841. The two uniquely talented individuals from French and English Canada respectively, shared a passion for parliamentary government and freedom. Working together, they planted the seeds that blossomed into one of the world's great democracies.

It is now over four centuries since the complex relations between a multitude of peoples and cultures have evolved within the confines of a vast, sometimes harsh, yet staggeringly beautiful land. The Canadian belief in social equality and the common good; the commitment to the principles of moderation, tolerance and inclusion, were all part of the constellation in which this nation was nurtured at the origins. The generations who came after travelled from all corners of the globe because that constellation cast a light which projected far beyond the gateway to freedom.

Canada in the New Millenium is a kaleidoscope of extraordinary images; a richly woven tapestry of diversity and pluralism. It is a gentle country where the accomodation of differences is the rule, not the exception.

Quite often, our federation surges with tension and with argument, and our regions variously progress and decline over time. Yet, in spite of our differences, Canadians share a lively understanding that ours is a nation conceived in the adventure of building a better place. But, as Professor Desmond Morton points out in the feature essay to follow: "our chief danger is that Canadians grow so preoccupied with the hyphens of their special identity that they forget the grandeur of it all."

Signal Hill, Newfoundland.

"Without rivers," Canadian novelist Hugh MacLennan wrote, "the early nation could never have survived."
(Shooting the Rapids, Frances Anne Hopkins)

"In the 18th century, parties of voyageurs and fur traders leaving Montreal paddled and portaged to the heart of the continent. They often travelled the routes developed by First Nations people in the birchbark canoes they had created. Explorers could push on by water to the mountains of the far West. West of the Rocky Mountains, rivers like the Fraser and the Columbia provided access to the Pacific Ocean. Rivers were the route the fur traders took into the Northwest Territories to set up trading posts.

Winding through or around formidable obstacles like dense forest, high mountain ranges and the impenetrable Shield, the waterways have been Canada's lifeline. Water gave Canadians east-west avenues across the country above the U.S. border and linked southern and northern Canada. "Without the rivers," Canadian novelist Hugh MacLennan observed, "the early nation could never have survived."

Perhaps our most powerful geographic feature is the St. Lawrence River, every inch of it, in Hugh MacLennan's magnificent phrase, "measured and brooded over by notaries and blessed by priests." It provides the great Canadian metaphor, defining the emotional difference between arriving on our shores and arriving on the American eastern seaboard, where you step from the wharf directly into the social and commercial heart of that country. "One enters Canada," Northrop Frye has written, "through the Strait of Belle Isle into the Gulf of St. Lawrence, where five Canadian provinces surround us, with enormous islands and glimpses of a mysterious mainland in the distance, but in the foreground only sea and sky. Then we go up the waterway of the St. Lawrence, which in itself is only the end of a chain of rivers and lakes that starts in the Rockies.... To enter the United States is a matter of crossing an ocean – to enter Canada is a matter of being silently swallowed by an alien continent." That 1,200-kilometre journey up the St. Lawrence, so quickly and blithely bypassed by the airlines, ought to be a requirement of Canadian citizenship. It was from the quays along this shoreline that the voyageurs set off along the rippling, rugged rivers that cleave the hinterland. They were in the service of the fur trade, the commerce that first gave substance to the notion of Canada as a transcontinental state. They crossed the Prairies and later the Rockies, claimed the watersheds of the Mississippi and Columbia and farmed up into the subarctic. They rode the great Churchill River, which roared down to Hudson Bay from the divide at Lac La Loche, site of the infamous Methye Portage, the longest and toughest on the trade routes. Conquering its 20-kilometre trail by climbing a 180-metre elevation under 40-kilogram packs of freight and furs earned voyageurs the ultimate badge of courage. After crossing this formidable rampart, the canoes were in Athabasca Country, whose gloomy forests eventually yielded the world's most prodigious fur catch.

The impact of these transcontinental trading routes was pervasive enough to work the magic that helped save Western Canada from being absorbed into the United States. Holding the land claimed through right of exploration, and later by occupation of the Hudson's Bay and North West companies, was a close call, but it was the scattering of those puny fur-trading outposts that held the line."

(Peter C. Newmann, in
Canada, the Land that Shapes Us).

"Canadians, new and old, are partners in a vast, beautiful and sometimes demanding country. They have resources and opportunities the rest of the world can envy. Our chief danger is that Canadians grow so preoccupied with the hyphens of their specific identity that they forget the grandeur of it all."

History as Controversy

History is a constructed artifact, built from particular memories and their interpretation. As in other countries, choosing Canada's memories and describing them is controversial. Canada's history is as divided as Canadians. In 1967, Canadians were encouraged to celebrate the centennial of Confederation; Québécois nationalists did so by tagging their car license plates, "cent ans d'injustice".

Canada's two official languages tend to purvey two very different views of our past. A phrase from Psalms, 72.8, "He shall have dominion also from sea unto sea" provided the founders of Confederation with a motto, a mari usque ad mare, and a description of their new creation but the word "Dominion", enshrined in Canada's constitution, soon became intolerable to Quebec, in part because it was identified as imperialist. Calling Canada a "kingdom" has not helped. The description of Canada as a nation, popular in 1867, became unacceptable because it overrode French Canada's claim to its own nationhood. Since the 1950s, French-speaking Quebeckers have relegated the phrase "French Canadian" to those who live outside Quebec, while Acadians insist on their distinct tradition. In a multicultural Canada, words like "race" and "ethnic" have become too sensitive for easy use. Aboriginal inhabitants, once described with wild geographic license as "Indians", now insist on being "First Nations"; references to their Asian ethnic roots, however genetically and archaeologically defensible, are resented by people who insist that aboriginal status is incompatible with any immigrant heritage.

Perhaps paradoxically, Canadians also believe that their history is boring; "as dull as ditchwater", claimed

Maurice Hutton at the turn of the century, or, claimed Claude Bissell, "a record of stolidity broken by bold imaginativeness". The dullness, to which generations of Canadian students often testify, may be deliberate. Except in Quebec, where history has served as a unifying national ideology, the clash of historical controversy has been muted to avoid offence. Sensitivities must be respected. Explorers and missionaries are harder to canonise now that Canadians understand that our First Nations did not ask to be "explored" and that they had gods of their own. It can be hard to honour Canada's sacrificial role in the two world wars of our century when Germans are Canada's fourth largest ethnic group and most Quebecois did not embrace the allied cause. The Darwinian image of a master race bred in Arctic cold and elemental struggle which comforted nineteenth century Canadian patriots is now properly out of fashion.

Regional Perspectives

Canada is a big country with a lot of different histories, some of them highly exclusive. Since provinces control the teaching of history, students are trained in regional grievances, many of them perpetrated by the federal politicians in Ottawa and the rest by the wealthy denizens of Canada's two central metropolises, Montreal and Toronto. French Canadians were traditionally assured in their manuals d'histoire that they were a people chosen of God, with a missionary role of spreading the Catholic faith to North America, leaving little comfort for natives, Protestants or even Irish Catholics. To this day a vigorous and painful debate rages in Quebec about whether one can become a true Quebecois or whether that honour is

Professor Desmond Paul Morton is the author of 36 books, an Officer of the Order of Canada, and Director of the McGill Institute for the Study of Canada.

reserved for the pures laines whose roots predate the British conquest in 1760.

Another perspective, identified with a Toronto historian, the late Donald Creighton, is the "Laurentian Thesis": that Canada was created by people with a transcontinental vision, willing to ignore distance, disappointment and derision to forge a country a mari usque ad mare. Such a vision of our history has heroes, villains and plenty of evidence of that "arduous destiny" that Edward Blake defined as Canada's noble fate. However Laurentianism offers no comfort to Quebecers, Westerners or any who were fainthearted or hostile to Creighton's heroes, Montreal's English-speaking entrepreneurs and the first post-Confederation prime minister, Sir John A.Macdonald (1867-1874, 1878-1891).

A more congenial theory, proposed by Maurice Careless and inspired by the graceful Liberal, Sir Wilfrid Laurier, the first French-Canadian prime minister (1896-1911), recognizes that Canadians have "limited identities", shaped by experience here or elsewhere into a hyphenated concept of themselves. Canadians are commonly defined by a string of identifying adjectives that provide a definition more revealing than their Social Insurance Number. Pierre Elliott Trudeau, a former prime minister (1968-1984), was a Quebec Catholic of French and Scottish ancestry. This complex identity, a product of history, reflects the vastness and conscious diversity of Canada and contributes to an image of fissiparousness and even imminent dissolution.

Yet what are the alternatives? Though Quebec nationalists claim their existence in Canada has been a failure, it has also been a dramatic success. The compromises of Confederation have consistently made it impossible for there to be a pan-Canadian conformity. The very process of managing difference led a Royal Commission on Biling-ualism and Biculturalism to become the reluctant ancestor of Canada's doctrine of multiculturalism. Its exemplars, oddly enough, were Icelanders who, by fleeing the volcanoes and poverty of their homeland, found themselves refugees in Manitoba in the 1870s. The community decided that their working language would be English but their culture would be proudly Icelandic. Such is the precedent for a Canada of many cultures and two official federal languages.

Getting Rich

Did Canadians ever have anything in common? One vulgar but honest proposition is that people came to Canada because they or their forebears wanted to get rich or, more accurately, to escape poverty. Why else did the first inhabitants cross the land bridge from Asia ten or twenty millennia ago? Why would more recent arrivals brave the terrible Atlantic crossing to come to a land that offered few of the balmy blessings of the South Seas? Canadians came to make as good a living as they could from the fishery, furs, forests and other staples. Their dream was to go home and the successful did so. In search of wealth, they trekked inland in search of fresh hunting grounds, deeper forests and more good land. Canadians still think of their harsh but beautiful northland as a source of future wealth.

The dominant theme in the economic history of Canada was first defined seventy years ago by Harold Innis. The search for wealth from staples explains Canada's enormous infrastructure of transportation and communications and the powerful corporations and government enterprises need-ed to make a Canadian economy work. And why apologize? To an impressive degree, in a hard country with a brutal climate, Canadians individually and collectively did find wealth, though some of them now wonder how ensuing generations will fare as well now that they know that even Canada's resources are finite and fast disappearing.

A Nation of Losers

Another harsh generality is that Canada has been populated by losers. Would the First Nations have come from Asia if they had triumphed in their old homeland? French Canadians, a defeated remnant in 1760, were abandoned by their own natural leaders who fled back to France. The los-

Over the ice of the St. Lawrence to and from Montréal, Québec, Francis George Coleridge.

The joy and sense of accomplishment of the Famous Five, honored for their courage in the struggle for gender equality, can be savoured at this larger-than-life monument on Parliament Hill.

Canoe manned by voyageurs passing a waterfall, Frances Anne Hopkins.

The historic abbey at St. Benoit du Lac in Québec's Eastern Townships.

Parliament at sunset.

Fathers of Confederation meeting at the Québec Conference, 1864.

ing side in the American War of Independence came north to establish the separate colonies of New Brunswick and Upper Canada (now Ontario). People displaced by the post-1815 depression in the British Isles led the way for waves of refugees from broken dreams – the Irish, Scots, Icelanders, Poles, Jews, Ukrainians, down to the Vietnamese boat people of the 1980s and the most recent fugitives from Eastern Europe's economic plight.

Losers have to go somewhere and they bring with them some discreet blessings. Harsh experience may make them a little more tolerant and cautious than the easily successful. Tolerance and prudence are virtues Canadians normally admire. They sometimes find them lacking in their success-oriented American neighbours. Canadians have bred people of strong opinions, from the Quebec nationalist Henri Bourassa to the upholder of constitutional tradition, Eugene Forsey, but they have excluded them from real power.

As Canadians, losers have turned into winners, though some feature of the Canadian character discourages boasting about the fact. Collectively, people have overcome hardships, discrimination and misfortune to gain prosperity and influence in their adopted land. Later generations have assimilated without losing homeland ties. Part of a common folk heritage warns that "rolling stones grow no moss" while praising those who have shown "get up and go".

A Separate Country

Canadians, as Winnipeg editor J.W. Dafoe used to remind them, are an American nation but they are not Americans. Two major British-American wars, in 1776-82 and 1812-14, helped define an international boundary. Confederation in 1867 confirmed the determination of Britain's North American colonies to live independently from the United States. At a cost, Canadians have kept the sovereign power to manage their own affairs. Those who objected to the cost (or perhaps merely the climate) could until recently easily become Americans. Canada remains the largest single source of American immigrants. On their own, Canadians have developed distinct institutions, from Parliament to public broadcasting and universal health insurance and perhaps a more robust sense of themselves than a dutiful emphasis on their differences would suggest.

The costs of being Canadian are not evenly shared. There are rich, poor and almost uninhabitable regions. Canadians crowd along their southern border and into cities. Canadians identify with geographic regions imperfectly identified with the ten provinces and two territories. The tidy-minded assume that small provinces (Prince Edward Island has only 112 thousand people) should amalgamate with their neighbours.

In 1864, delegates from the three Maritime colonies met in Charlottetown to discuss union. Delegates from the distant Canadas soon convinced them that it would be easier to create a transcontinental nation than to reconcile Maritime differences. After all, each small colony had a distinct history. New Brunswick was split between its hardscrabble Protestant farmers in the south and French-speaking Acadians on the north shore. Prince Edward Island was still preoccupied with the depredations of its absentee landlords. Newfoundland's merchant princes recoiled from contact with Canada; their capital, St. John's, was closer to London than to Ottawa.

Little has changed. Provincial rivalries cloak internal regionalism. Cape Breton despises the Nova Scotia mainland; British Columbia's interior suspects the Lower Mainland of immoral greed. Ontario's North would cheerfully secede from the South if only the North's own regions

*Parliamentary Library
With Statue of
D'Arcy McGee.*

could agree on anything else. The greedy rivalry of
Edmonton and Calgary leaves less favoured regions of
Alberta resentful. The forty-five thousand people of the
Northwest Territories demand division into Nunavut and
Denendeh. Yukon's 9,000 natives are divided in seven dis-
tinct nations, each with its own language and overlapping
land claims. A former prime minister, William Lyon
Mackenzie King (1921-1930, 1935-1948), once claimed
that Canada had too much geography. Obviously there is
not enough to satisfy the inhabitants.

Provincial Rights

How, in the face of such centrifugal forces, did the idea of
Confederation ever prevail? In part, it was one of those
instances of "bold imaginativeness" recalled by the late
Claude Bissell, president of the University of Toronto. The
United Province of Canada – now Ontario and Quebec – was
trapped in a political stalemate of conservatives and reform-
ers, rouges and bleus. The four Atlantic colonies were suffo-
cating in their smallness. Britain, in the grip of imperial pes-
simism, wanted to leave her British North American colonies
in a sufficiently durable arrangement that she could retreat in
dignity before a probable American take-over. Sharp-eyed

politicians and businessmen – Creighton's heroes – wanted a
common market and a regime strong enough to occupy the
vast western properties of the Hudson's Bay Company before
the Yankees grabbed them.

The architects of Confederation devised a powerful central government, armed with every power needed to secure
"peace, order and good government" – a slogan of Canadian
government that contrasts almost deliberately with the
American goal of "life, liberty and the pursuit of happiness".
Provinces, Macdonald suggested, would be hardly more
than municipal institutions, responsible for the few dirt
roads, one-room schools and "charitable and eleemosynary
institutions". French Canadians reluctantly concurred, in
part because their spokesman, Sir George-Etienne Cartier
insisted, with much prescience, that provincial powers
would protect their "cultural nationality", in part because
they expected their political skills would suffice to domi-
nate the new regime as they shrewdly managed the old
United Province. Nova Scotia and New Brunswick were
forced into Confederation by a mixture of fear of the United
States and pressure from Britain. Prince Edward Island
joined only after railway bankruptcy; Newfoundland stayed
out until 1949.

How frail is the prophetic vision. Within a few decades Macdonald's "municipal institutions" have been transformed, thanks to British judges, into regimes fully sovereign in their own range of powers. Provincial politicians have discovered that fighting Ottawa is the easiest way to gain votes. Roads, health care, welfare and education have become the greatest responsibilities of any government in an urbanized technological society. To retain power, reinforce provincial allies and recognize the shift in financial burdens, the central government has sacrificed much of the fiscal leverage it gained in 1867. Canada has become so highly decentralized a federal system that the main issue of the 1990s is whether it can stop short of disintegration.

Le fait français

Regionalism, provincial rights, inequities of wealth and opportunity would be preoccupations enough for any middle-rank power but another theme dominates our history: French-English relations. Like a fire in a peatbog, they are sometimes merely warm under foot; occasionally they flame in the skies. They explain Canada's caution in world affairs and her decentralization at home. Quebec makes Confederation possible and difficult at the same time. Because Quebec, like any wise minority, is monolithic in its preferences, it has almost always sat with the government, deftly switching sides in 1896 and 1984 when party dominance shifted. Members of the fractured majority have often complained that their own preoccupations are set aside to satisfy this shrewd but insatiable population.

What does Quebec want? The answer, simply put, is survival – "la survivance" – for a language and culture enormously outnumbered on this continent. For generations that goal was sought through a robust if sometimes opportune Catholicism, a conservative, corporatist social philosophy and the acceptance of poverty and ruralism for most Canadiens as a fair price for a culture and the promise of paradise. That acceptance faded in the 1940s when Canada emerged as a major winner of the Second World War into an era of unprecedented prosperity. By the 1960s Quebec had switched from the Church to the State as the prime instrument of survival. L'Etat du Québec could deliver power and pride but only to Québécois. French-Canadians outside Quebec were beyond its reach. While the Church had never challenged English as the working language of business in Quebec, the State could. While Ottawa imposed official bilingualism on federal services and tried to persuade provinces to follow suit, Quebec proceeded to abolish English as a public language and, within a few years, made French the language of business and industry. A decade after Québécois had rejected even the possibility of negotiating for sovereignty and association with Canada, most Quebeckers appeared serenely confident that their new commercial expertise would guarantee them a prosperous independence.

Canada in the World

The French fact has particularly shaped Canada's role in the world, resisting what Carl Berger described as "imperial nationalism" at the turn of the century when some Canadians saw their destiny as pillars and future rulers of the British Empire. French Canada opposed Canada's contribution to the Boer War and helped sink a Canadian navy in 1911 for fear it would be a pawn of the British fleet. Quebec soon withdrew from the national crusade when Canada joined the British war effort in 1914 and bitterly fought conscription when it was opposed in 1917. The war left Canada with an enhanced identity and the means to achieve full national sovereignty but the cost – 60,000 dead and as many permanently disabled, persuaded many Canadians that French-Canadian isolationism had much to commend it. Fears for national unity made Canada an opponent of the League of Nations' timid approach to collective security and a cheerful backer of appeasement in the 1930s – at least until Britain went to war again in 1939 and Canada followed a week later.

For Canada, the Second World War was a far greater but less painful struggle. Once again, conscription became a bitter issue between French and English but a concentration on war in the air and at sea and on wartime production limited the manpower crisis to the army and few conscripts saw action. In the postwar world split between the United States and the Soviet Union, British loyalties became less relevant and Canada, as a rich middle power, could speak with its own national voice provided it was not too out of tune with its American neighbour. Indeed Ottawa sought international roles in the United Nations and the North Atlantic Treaty Organization (NATO) as a means of diversifying a potentially stifling bilateral embrace with the United States.

In *Lament for a Nation*, published in 1965, the philosopher George Grant predicted that such efforts were unavailing. By wholeheartedly seeking an American standard of living and defeating a Conservative government that had rejected American guidance during the 1962 Cuban missile crisis, only political inertia would delay the inevitable disintegration of Canada and its ultimate absorbtion in the United States. Whether Americans would want Canada would be decided in Washington; given that the United States could get all it wanted economically, acceptance was by no means certain. This gloomy view could be sustained by the failure, in the Trudeau years, to persuade Canadian business to develop substantial multilateral trade links and by the Mulroney government's conversion and total commitment to a wide-ranging free-trade agreement with the United States.

It was less the Free Trade agreement than higher taxes, an uncontrolled federal deficit and fumbled attempts to find a constitutional formula that satisfied both Quebec and the rest of Canada that almost annihilated Mulroney's party in 1993. The Liberals returned under Jean Chrétien,

"Maples are such sociable trees," said Anne of Green Gables. "They are always rustling and whispering to you."

a devout federalist and veteran politician who had held almost every cabinet portfolio under Pierre Trudeau. At a high cost to Canada's social policies, Chrétien curbed the deficit, changed his mind to favour Free Trade, identified closely with President Bill Clinton of the United States and outlasted Quebec sovereignists, despite a 1995 referendum that brought the Yes side to 49.4 per cent of the vote. Canadians grumbled about high taxes and a dollar worth US $0.65, but they reflected on the alternatives and grudgingly gave Chrétien three successive parliamentary majorities. The rest split their votes among four parties, most of them defined by region. Almost half refused to vote.

Canadian prospects

Like journalists, historians specialize in bad news. It appears to be more entertaining and there is more of it. Regional, cultural and linguistic differences may be uncomfortable but they are the important unifying themes of our history. However important our official embrace of multiculturalism or our more recent venture into multiracialism, or relations with Canada's original peoples may be, it is French-English relations that have the current potential to dissolve Confederation. Yet the chronic gloom that seems to

hang over northern countries can deceive. Canadians are divided because nothing terrifies them into unity. They have more in common than the climate and a tendency to mumble in both official languages. Only two federal systems in the world are older and both the Swiss and the Americans fought bloody civil wars to stay together.

Despite George Grant's predictions, the inevitable seldom happens. National sovereignty can co-exist with regional trading arrangements even on the scale of the Canada-U.S. Free Trade Agreement or the European Economic Community. Canadians have a democratic political system: if their leaders fail them or even grow wearisome, they are replaced. There are national traditions of civility, tolerance and co-operation which, imperfectly, set the standards for civil conduct. There are national institutions and memories which create a Canadian identity that spans the fissures of language, culture and region.

Canadians, new and old, are partners in a vast, beautiful and sometimes demanding country. They have resources and opportunities the rest of the world can envy. Our chief danger is that Canadians grow so preoccupied with the hyphens of their specific identity that they forget the grandeur of it all.

After the Ice Storm.

One of the World's Oldest Dem

cracies Celebrates Canada Day

The Hall of Honour at Christmas.

Photo from one of ten Tourist Attraction Commemorative Stamps launched on May 11, 2001 at the Canadian Tulip Festival, Ottawa.

Canada's Constitutional Framework

After a number of debates in the 1860s concerning language, federalism, minority rights, and the threat of absorption by the United States, Canada's "Fathers of Confederation" decided on what kind of constitution Canada should have. They drafted a blueprint for a new federal state in the British North America Act (BNA Act) which was passed by the British Parliament in 1867. Over one hundred years later, upon its patriation from Britain to Canada, the BNA Act was renamed the Constitution Act, 1867.

It is an axiom of Canadian parliamentary democracy that a government cannot be accountable to itself. Canadians believe that governments should be limited by a Constitution. This principle, called constitutionalism, limits the organization, conduct, and powers of governments in a written constitution as well as by unwritten customs and traditions that have become entrenched in the Constitution. The principle is extremely important because it makes the Constitution supreme above all government institutions, public policies, and politics itself.

The Constitution Act, 1867 is the symbol of Canada's regal, legal and political diversities. For Canadians, it is the highest secular law, containing the important principles of federalism and parliamentary democracy. It is the first law of the land, the law from which all other laws originate and the law to which all national and international laws, must conform. Canada's effective constitution is said to have both written and unwritten features.

There have been two major influences on the development of Canada's constitution. First, from the British tradition, more than one statutory document has constitutional significance in Canada. Canada follows many similar unwritten British constitutional traditions and conventions, such as the role of the prime minister, cabinet and political parties in Parliament, the solidarity of the Cabinet and the rules of debate. Second, from the United States tradition, the most substantive aspects of the Canadian constitution are written and entrenched with rigorous amending formulae.

When Canada was created by an act of the British Parliament in 1867, there was no mention of the substantive rights of Canadians in that document. They were assumed to exist as part of the legal tradition Canadians inherited from Britain dating back to the Magna Carta in 1215. After years of discussion, debate and fierce argument, the provincial premiers and the government of Pierre Elliot Trudeau finally agreed on the Canadian Charter of Rights and Freedoms, which became a permanent part of Canada's patriated Constitution in 1982.

The Canadian Charter of Rights and Freedoms contains no less than 34 sections that protect the constitutional rights of Canadians. There are substantive rights that specify a condition of freedom and advantage that can be enjoyed for its own sake. These freedoms include, conscience, belief, religion, thought, opinion and expression; the press and other media communication; and peaceful assembly and association. Other protected rights are procedural rights, democratic rights, mobility rights, legal rights and equality rights.

The Constitution Act, 1867, made Canada the first nation-state to combine principles of federalism with parliamentary institutions. According to the constitution, the powers of government are divided and shared by the federal and provincial governments which make their laws in parliaments based on the Westminister model. Accordingly, when Canadians speak of their constitution, they mean the whole system of government in Canada, that is, parliamentary and

PARLIAMENTARY GOVERNMENT

Dr. James J. Guy is a Professor of Political Science at the University College of Cape Breton and an author of a number of well received books on government and politics.

Canada's breathtaking Library of Parliament under moonlight.

powers, whereby the political executive (prime minister and cabinet) and legislative institutions are fused. According to this fundamental parliamentary principle, the Prime Minister and every other minister must by custom and convention be a member of the House of Commons or the Senate, or gain a seat in one House or the other within a short time of appointment.

Parliament plays many important roles. In addition to its legislative functions, it has several nonlegislative functions: it can propose certain amendments to the Constitution, it participates in the declaration of war, it scrutinizes all government finances through the Auditor General, it regulates the conduct of its Members, and can punish, censure, and expel them. Very important is the ability of Parliament to educate Canadians about new issues as they appear on the political agenda. The media attention paid to Parliament gives it the opportunity to draw the public's attention to problems that need some form of governmental action.

The Sovereign

Canada is a constitutional monarchy, which means that it is a democracy headed by a king or a queen. The Canadian constitution affirms that executive authority is vested in the monarch and exercised by his or her appointed representatives, the governor general, and the lieutenant governors. The monarch serves as a symbol of national sovereignty for Canadians. In 1947, the functions of the monarch as head of state were delegated to the governor general. However, in practice the governor general usually plays a passive executive role by following the advice of the prime minister and the cabinet.

Under the Canadian constitution, the governor general has the right to be consulted, to advise, and even to warn

cabinet government, the federal system, provincial legislatures, the rule of law and democracy.

Parliamentary Institutions

The Parliament of Canada has three components: The Queen, who is the head of state (represented by the Governor General when the monarch is not in Canada), the Senate and the House of Commons. Ultimately, Parliament is supreme because it is the national lawmaking body.

While the Queen and her representative, the Governor General, comprise the head of state, the prime minister is the head of government. The prime minister chooses the cabinet, known collectively as the government, which is made up of the prime minister and all those appointed as ministers of the Crown. Over the years, the cabinet has differentiated itself from Parliament, placing itself in the dominant position to control the law-making process, to determine legislative proceedings, and to plan the general order of business members of parliament will consider. Government bills are rarely defeated in parliament because the governing party almost always musters a majority of its legislative supporters in favour of its legislation.

Parliamentary government in Canada is based on the fusion of

Changing of the Guard.

The Mace is the symbol of parliamentary authority.

House of Commons In Session, 2001.

the political executive if they abuse their powers. The governor general summons Parliament, brings its sessions to a close, and dissolves Parliament before an election. As the representative of the monarch, the governor general signs all bills, conferring royal assent before they become law. The governor general also delivers the Speech from the Throne at the opening of a session, outlining the government's legislative plans.

The office of governor general is the oldest continuous institution in Canada, representing Canada's evolution as a colony to an independent state within the international system. The governor general has two official residences, Rideau Hall in Ottawa, and La Citadelle in Quebec City. When members of the Royal Family visit Canada, they stay at these residences. Other heads of state and dignitaries are also guests.

The Canadian House of Commons

The popularly elected House of Commons is the centre-piece of Canada's Parliamentary system of government. It is the central legislative link between the public and the government in Canadian democracy; it is where elected representatives meet daily in open verbal combat to debate and make decisions about the issues of national politics.

The House of Commons plays three vital roles in Canada's parliamentary system. One is that of federal lawmaker, making public policies that govern the country. The second role is local representation, articulating the viewpoints of the various interests in Canadian society and securing tangible benefits for individual ridings. The third is that of a forum for debating the major political and governmental concerns of Canadians.

The basic principle of representation in the House of Commons is that each province is represented in proportion to its population. Thus the 301 seats in the Commons are distributed among the provinces in the following manner: Ontario, 103; Quebec, 75; British Columbia, 34; Alberta, 26; Manitoba, 14; Saskatchewan, 14; Nova Scotia, 11; New Brunswick, 10; Newfoundland, 7; Prince Edward Island, 4; Northwest Territories, 2; and Yukon, 1.

According to Canadian constitutional law, the House of Commons exercises some fundamental powers that have profound democratic importance. One is that when a bill is proposed it must be approved by a majority of elected Members of Parliament before it becomes the law of the land. Another is that the House of Commons has the power to carefully examine all matters involving the raising and spending of money by the government.

Each Member of Parliament represents the people of a specific constituency or riding. Collectively, the House of Commons consists of 301 elected members and is responsible for most of the legislation introduced in Parliament. Both Members of the House of Commons and Senators are Members of Parliament. But the term 'M.P.' is usually used to refer to the elected Members of the House of Commons.

The House of Commons is politically important because its party composition is the basis for the formation of the federal government. It enables the leaders of one political party to govern with a majority or minority of members' support and it enables other political parties to observe and oppose government and provide alternatives to its policies.

The pomp and ceremony of parliamentary government is central to the proceedings of the House of Commons. Each sitting day begins with the Speaker's parade, a ceremonial procession that highlights the Speaker, who wears black robes and is escorted to the Chamber by the Sergeant-at Arms, who carries the mace, which is the symbol of parliamentary authority.

The Senate In Session, 2001.

The Senate

The Senate is Canada's unelected upper house of Parliament. All legislation must pass through the Senate before it becomes law.

Its members are appointed by the Governor General on the recommendation of the Prime Minister. The opening of Parliament, the Royal Assent to Bills and the Prorogation (ending of a session) of Parliament take place in the Senate Chamber. On these occasions, the Speaker and Members of the House of Commons attend at the Bar of the Senate Chamber after being duly summoned to do so.

Unlike the composition of the House of Commons which is based on representation by population, the composition of the Senate is based on the principle of regional representation. This regional representation is central to the role of the Senate in Canada's system of government and the Chamber serves as a forum for the expression of regional concerns.

There are 105 Senators under the following provincial and regional representations: Ontario, 24; Quebec 24; 10 each for Nova Scotia and New Brunswick, 6 each for British Columbia, Alberta, Saskatchewan, Manitoba and Newfoundland; Prince Edward Island, 4; and one each for Yukon, the Northwest Territories, and Nunavut.

Senators cannot introduce tax bills or bills to spend money, although they can block their passage once they have come out of the House of Commons. But bills can be introduced in the Senate which can sometimes result in important contributions to Canadian public policy.

In effect the Senate has almost identical powers to the House of Commons. And, no federal bill can become law without the Senate's consent. The Senate can veto any legislation from the Commons as often as it wants, including budget bills, although it has not done so very often because it is an appointed legislative body.

The Senate cannot prevent its own abolition. The Constitution provides that the Senate can be abolished or changed by the House of Commons and the consent of seven provinces representing 50 percent of the national population. The Senate can only delay constitutional amendments for up to 180 days.

The Senate plays an active research role through its special committees and the results of that work have had a major impact on government programs and legislation. Because of the experience of Senators, Senate committees possess considerable expertise in improving the legal and technical wording of complicated bills. The Senate is able to conduct special public inquiries into pressing political issues, such as its studies on mandatory retirement, and the mass media. In fact, special Senate Committees have produced a number of extensive and diverse reports covering a wide range of issues of importance to Canadians, including Canada's foreign policy, children and poverty; and Canada's positioning in the technological revolution.

But because it is an unelected body, the Senate does not share the popular acceptance accorded to the House of Commons. As a result, many Canadians have called for reforms to Parliament's upper house.

Discover Our True Nature

Air Ballooning over the Ottawa River.

Mont Tremblant, Québec.

Cavendish Beach, Prince Edward Island.

Fireworks in Montréal.

Canada's geographic grandeur and spectacular scenery have been the subject of awed testimony going back thousands of years to the legends, myths and stories of the First Nations. The modern tourist is generally equally captivated, but often overwhelmed by the vast open spaces and the nordicity of a place which often seems much more of a continent than a country.

In fact, the landscape is a collage of different environments – mountain, prairie, forest, farmland, marine and tundra – spread over 10 million square kilometers in ten provinces and three territories.

The second largest geographical area in the world, Canada is a country of 30.5 million people with two official languages, English and French. Canadians make up a generally prosperous and cosmopolitan population with a richly diverse cultural composition. They form an ethnic mosaic as diverse as the land itself. More than ninety distinct cultural groups, from Aboriginals through descendants of French and British pioneers, to recent immigrants from Asia and Latin America, constitute the social fabric.

Along with the international linkages which are so obviously byproducts of Canada's multiculturalism, proximity to the United States is a major influence on tourism development and patterns. Canada is the nearest international destination for the majority of the US population. The converse is true for Canadians: most live within 250 kilometres of the US border.

Canada's tourism products compare favorably with those of its international competition, with key strengths in those that relate closely to its scenic natural resources. The incomparable wilderness settings of Banff, in the Province of Alberta, Auyuittuq National Park in the newly created Territory of Nunavut, and the mighty Nahanni River in the Northwest Territories, provide only a few striking examples. World renowned popular resorts such as Québec's Mont Tremblant and British Columbia's skiing paradise at Whistler only begin to touch the sur-

By Jim Watson, former President & C.E.O., Canadian Tourism Commission; with Scott Meis and Oliver Martin.

Lake Louise, Banff National Park, Alberta.

Baddeck, Nova Scotia Regatta.

Québec Winter Carnival Ice Canoe Races.

Royal Hudson Train Excursion, British Columbia.

face of Canada's natural treasure house.

Urban centers which include Toronto, Montréal, Vancouver or the nation's capital, Ottawa are gracious, largely crime free, and interesting Canadian cities. They possess varied and sophisticated cultural attractions, lovely natural parks, and sports facilities always close at hand, along with the rich diversity of populations which are often microcosms of the world at large.

According to the World Tourism Organization (2000), Canada accounts for 2.9 percent of international tourist arrivals and 2.3 percent of receipts. In 2000, Canada earned $10.8 billion from sales of both goods and services to 20.4 million international visitors, making tourism one of the most important exports for the country.

US visitors account for about 78 percent of foreign arrivals. While the number of Americans visiting Canada has increased modestly in recent years, their market share has dropped considerably from the 1970s when they accounted for almost 90 percent of all international arrivals. By contrast, Asian market shares, especially from Japan, Taiwan, and South Korea, have been rising rapidly. Increases in European market share have not been as great as from Asia, but Europe, especially the United Kingdom, France and Germany remains an important market for Canada.

In 2000, Canadians spent about $15.5 billion on purchases of both goods and services involving 19.2 million international visits, making tourism one of the most important imports for the country. About 80 percent of all Canadians visit the United States, although this percentage is slowly declining in favour of outbound visits to other destinations. (in part due to the relative wealth of Canadian tourists, particularly the baby boom market segment.) In recent years, the tourism account balance – the difference between expenditures by Canadians going abroad and receipts from foreigners – has declined. In 1992, the deficit was over $6 billion; in 1999, it was $1.7 billion.

While international tourism is important, domestic tourism far exceeds it in economic significance. Approximately 70 percent of all tourism spending in Canada comes from domestic tourism receipts. The small ratio of international to domestic, is due in large part to the size of Canada and its domestic attractions. Eco-tourism and the marvels of the outdoor recreation opportunities awaiting tourists, no matter what their interests, are principal reasons why Canadians choose more and more to discover their own country.

The tourism industry is a major component of the Canadian economy. For example, total tourism spending in 2000 was $54.1 billion, up 7.9 per cent from 1999. Tourism's resulting total direct effect on the economy was estimated at $21.8 billion, up 2.4 percent over 1999. Employment estimates also indicate that tourism job creation growth has exceeded that in the overall business sector.

In another vein, tourism in Canada has a well-developed social infrastructure with many different public and private sector organizations including government departments, trades, industry advocacy groups, destination marketing organizations and other tourism bodies at all levels. Within the public sector, the federal, provincial or territorial governments share roles and responsibilities in respect to tourism.

The two most influential organizations at the national level are the Canadian Tourism Commission (CTC) and the Tourism Industry Association of Canada (TIAC). The CTC is a national partnership between the industry and all levels of government in Canada. The CTC is a federal Crown Corporation that in 2000 received approximately $81 million from the federal government to market Canada as a tourism destination.

The TIAC is a national advocacy organization that promotes the interests of Canadian tourism by formulating and advocating policies and programmes to the federal government.

Despite this progress and commitment, Canada's tourism industry faces numerous challenges. Two of the most significant are changing market demographics, and increased international competition.

All Canada's main markets (domestic Canadians, Americans, Europeans and Japanese) have aging populations. Matching the different product interests of this growing senior citizen segment will require changes in many existing products and services, in addition to developing new ones.

Moreover, international competition continues to intensify. In response, Canada has introduced a number of new trade facilitation initiatives. Significant interventions include the creation of the Canadian Tourism Commission, the historic Open Skies agreement between Canada and the USA, and new arrangements to facilitate the move-

Totem Pole, British Columbia.

ment of tourists on the ground as well as at major air terminals.

Canada's tourism industry faces the twenty-first century with a new positive attitude of confidence and determination arising out of the emergence of a strong sense of common national vision. Industry partnership and national leadership support are both important stimulants to a thriving, dynamic, and imaginative industry.

But the most important factor is the product itself. In Canada, the traveller finds respite from a crowded, noisy planet. Here, one finds space and enormity, silence and abundance. Thousands of shimmering lakes and forests of whispering maples await the visitor. So, too, do ancient rain forests and fascinating coastlines. That huge blue sky over the prairies and the adventure of Canada's Arctic expanses are just waiting to be explored.

Discover our true nature. Witness the majesty of our mountains and savour the golden twilight over old Montréal. Explore the endless sunsets of our Atlantic provinces and the wonders of the Yukon. Take the time to discover and rediscover the generous, gentle land of the Red Maple Leaf. And in that discovery, make a part of Canada yours forever!

Québec National Assembly, Québec City.

Hartland Covered Bridge, New Brunswick. It is the longest covered bridge in the world.

The Nova Scotia International Tattoo is the world's largest annual indoor show and is held in Halifax.

Beulach Bann Falls, Cape Breton.

Windsurfing is a national passion.

Alcan – An aerial view of the $93 million anode paste plant commissioned by Alcan as part of a 10 year, $400 million environmental improvement initiative aimed at reducing smelter emissions.

Editor's Note. We have illustrated the text with photos of some Canadian owned and Canadian based companies which are making a difference – both in terms of the ingenuity of their product lines, their commitments to environmental and social responsibilities, and as employers who put people first. Space limitations give us only a small taste of the genius and innovation of the Canadian people, but we hope the reader will, given this sampling of companies from coast to coast, large and small, want to know more about doing business in one of the most dynamic economies on earth.

Silicon Island – Sydney, Cape Breton's Silicon Island Art and Innovation Centre was one of the first Information Technology clusters in Canada and houses fifteen businesses involved in IT, digital media, and cultural and heritage pursuits. This nurturing, productive space – located in the beautifully restored former County Court House – showcases one of Cape Breton's fastest-growing sectors, the knowledge-based industry.

Economic Size and Development

Canada is the second-largest country in the world in terms of land area (almost 10 million square kilometres), but has a relatively small population of 30.5 million. A member of the Organisation for Economic Co-operation and Development (OECD) and the Group of Seven (G-7), Canada is one of the most advanced industrialized nations. It is the eighth-largest economy in terms of gross domestic product (GDP), with per capita purchasing power second only to that of the United States. Canada consistently performs well in terms of social indicators. For example, the United Nations has ranked Canada first on its Human Development Index over the last decade, only recently placing the country in a still very impressive third place in a list comprising 174 states.

Structure of the Economy

Although Canada is rich in natural resources, which have historically played an important role in its economic development, the service sector has been the mainstay of the economy since the turn of the twentieth century. The service sector has employed more people than primary industries and has been the number-one contributor to GDP since the early 1920s. Today, three out of four Canadians are employed in this sector, which generates about three-

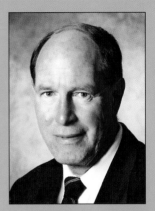

Mr. David Dodge is the Governor of the Bank of Canada

THE ECONOMY

Bank of Canada, Ottawa.

quarters of Canada's GDP.

Canada has long had an open economy and has always relied heavily on international trade and investment. Today, more than 40 percent of Canada's output is exported, up from 25 percent a decade ago. While, more than 80 percent of Canada's foreign trade is with the United States, the European Union and Japan are also important trading partners. The composition of Canada's exports has shifted away from primary industries (which now make up only 35 percent of total exports, compared with 50 percent in 1992) towards manufactured goods and services. Foreign direct investment in Canada supports more than half of all Canadian exports, and three out of ten Canadian jobs.

Economic Policies and Reform

The importance of international trade has been reinforced by policies that promote trade. The 1994 North American Free Trade Agreement (NAFTA) (between Canada, the United States, and Mexico), which superseded the Canada-U.S. Free Trade Agreement (FTA) of 1989, is a cornerstone of Canadian trade policy.

Canada also has free-trade agreements with Chile and Israel, and is involved in other regional economic co-operation initiatives, such as the Asia Pacific Economic Cooperation (APEC) forum and the embryonic Free Trade Area of the Americas (FTAA). In addition, Canada is a strong supporter of global trade liberalization, particularly in the context of the World Trade Organization (WTO). Indeed, the establishment of the WTO as a permanent institution was a Canadian proposal, approved by international consensus during the Uruguay Round of the General Agreement on Tariffs and Trade (GATT).

Increased trade liberalization has led to a wave of private sector restructuring over the past decade, aimed at cutting production costs and increasing efficiency and competitiveness. While restructuring initially caused some declines in employment and output, the rationalization of business lines and the utilization of new technologies and production processes have since been paying off in terms of higher output and employment.

Canada's public sector also under-

National Research Council (NRC)

Dr. Bob Walkow lit by the viewing port of the scanning tunneling microscope. He is at the forefront of current research in the fast growing field of nanotechnology.

From Discovery to Innovation: Science at Work for Canada

The NRC is Canada's foremost science and technology research agency. It works not only to develop new knowledge and technology, but also to help transform discoveries into new products and services. In this way, the NRC supports Canadian firms, helps create jobs, fuels economic growth through increased competitiveness, and contributes to a higher quality of life for Canadians.

NRC has both a global reach and a local touch. It is a key catalyst in research and development partnerships and collaborations with universities, governments and businesses, at home and internationally. One of its priorities is to develop Canada's innovation system and support sustained economic growth in regions and communities across the nation.

NRC's research institutes, with their top-flight facilities and staff, are the core of its innovation effort. Strategic long-term investments are made in a wide range of R&D fields most relevant to Canada's knowedge-based economy. The goal is to connect NRC's core research strengths and its knowledge and technical support networks with the commercial development and product-oriented activities of Canadian industry.

went serious restructuring in the 1990s, as a result of which the fiscal positions of most levels of government have improved significantly. The federal government moved into a position of fiscal surplus in 1997, which has allowed it to start paying down the national debt while also introducing tax cuts and targeted increases in spending.

Canada's monetary policy regime has also been strengthened with the introduction of explicit inflation targets in 1991. These targets, jointly agreed to by the government and the Bank of Canada, were designed to bring inflation down from the high levels experienced in the 1970s and 1980s, and to keep it low and stable-currently within a range of 1 to 3 percent. Since 1991, inflation has consistently remained within the target range.

Recent Economic Developments

Through the early 1990s, Canada's economic performance was relatively weak, reflecting the effects of the adjustments that were necessary to deal with high inflation and to restructure the private and public sectors. Since then, however, the sounder foundations resulting from these adjustments have supported a strong economic performance. These foundations have allowed the economy to weather the turbulence caused by the Asian financial crisis and the Russian debt default during 1997 to 1998 and to continue to grow through that period.

Another factor behind the solid performance of the Canadian economy in recent years has been the strong, sustained economic expansion in the United States, which has

Ballard Technologies of British Columbia and Xcellis concluded successful two-year field trials of fuel cell buses in 2000. Three buses operated with the Chicago Transit Agency and others operated with Translink in Vancouver. Free of noxious exhaust, these vehicles are very quiet in comparison with buses powered by internal combustion engines.

Dr. Garth Fletcher of Aqua-Bounty holds a transgenic salmon (containing an antifreeze promoter linked to a salmon growth hormone gene) with a standard control salmon for comparison. Both salmon are two years old.

bolstered demand for Canadian products.

Altogether, the Canadian economy is in good shape going into the new millennium. Against a backdrop of improved fiscal health, low and stable inflation, relatively low interest rates, and growing employment and incomes, it should continue to grow at a solid pace, providing the basis for improved standards of living.

Economic indicators	1995	1996	1997	1998	1999
GDP (Can$, billions)*	807.1	833.1	877.9	901.8	957.9
GDP per capita	27,495	28,076	29,277	29,815	31,416
Real GDP growth (%)	2.8	1.5	4.4	3.3	4.5
CPI inflation	2.2	1.6	1.6	0.9	1.7
Bank Rate	7.2	4.7	3.5	5.2	4.9
Unemployment rate	9.4	9.6	9.1	8.3	7.6
Exports of goods and services	391.8	399.0	401.7	422.8	433.6
Imports of goods and services	376.8	374.2	376.9	388.9	403.8
Total business investment (% GDP)	40.2	40.8	47.5	49.2	48.9
Total public debt (% GDP)**	88.5	88.2	83.4	81.4	75.3

Notes:

Current Can$ figures are used in all calculations, except where otherwise indicated. Public debt includes federal, provincial, and local debt, as well as Quebec Pension Plan and Canada.

The Honorable Paul Martin is the former Minister of Finance.

Mr. Martin recently outlined Canada's strengths in the knowledge-based economy to an enthusiastic audience in New York.

"Let me give you some examples of how Canada measures up. We have the highest percentage of our population online of any country in the world. Canada was the first to connect all of its schools and libraries to the Internet. We have the highest per capita ownership of home computers and the widest access to cable systems in the world. We have built the world's fastest and most advanced optical internet, which is revolutionizing telecommunications technology. Canadian universities are home to 8 of the top 20 electrical engineering programs in North America, and 7 of the top 20 computer engineering schools – not bad for a country one-tenth the size of the U.S.! Our labour force has the highest proportion of people with post-secondary education in the world.

At the same time, we have fundamentally changed the Government's role in the economy. The federal government once owned Canada's largest airline, a major oil company, a major railroad – and the list went on. This is no longer the case. What we have done is refocus our energy on those areas where the Government's role is essential. For example, we have just made the most significant investment ever in our publicly funded health care system.

Looking ahead to the demands of the knowledge economy, and despite having one of the most attractive R & D tax credit regimes in the world, we identified R & D as an area in which Canada needed to play catch-up.

Three years ago we created the Canada Foundation for Innovation – one of the largest of its kind in the world – to boost the research infrastructure in our universities, colleges and research hospitals.

In the last year we established 2,000 new research chairs in Canadian universities to attract and retain the best researchers in the world.

This year we launched 13 new world-leading institutes in areas such as cancer, aging and children's health to maximize the advantage Canada enjoys in medical research.

And to better develop the remarkable promise that lies in biotechnolo-

Genome Research.

Innovation Place is one of the most rapidly growing, and most successful university-related research parks in North America. Located in Saskatoon, Saskatchewan, Innovation Place builds on the strengths of the university in agriculture, information technologies, resources and the life sciences, contributing over $195 million to the economy of Saskatoon and Saskatchewan.

gy and genetics, we have launched Genome Canada, which is building five world-leading centres of genomic research across our country.

We also needed to take action in terms of our tax system, and that is happening. Recently, we implemented a $100-billion tax cut package – the largest in Canada's history – lowering taxes on individuals, entrepreneurs and corporations. Personal income taxes have been cut at all income levels. On average, they have dropped by 21 percent, even more for middle-income Canadians with children.

Moreover, we have decided to create a distinct Canadian advantage in the crucial areas of capital investment and global competitiveness.

The capital gains tax rate in Canada, averaging 23 percent, is now lower than it is in the United States.

Canada's taxation of stock options is now more generous and flexible than it is in the U.S.

And finally, the average corporate tax rate for business in Canada is

falling to 32 percent – almost 5 percentage points lower than U.S. rates.

The net effect of all this is a Canada prepared to succeed and poised to surprise. In short, the Canada of today is at the leading edge of the economy of tomorrow.

This reality differs substantially from how some people may perceive our country. Indeed, our vast geography, scenic vistas and rich natural environment have helped to perpetuate the notion that our economy is overwhelmingly based on resource and commodity production. But today that view of Canada is as outdated as saying that New York's economy is based on the garment industry, or the economy of Chicago is based on the railway.

Our trade numbers tell an important part of the story. Commodities as a share of exports have fallen from almost 60 percent in 1980 to about 30 percent in 1999. In the year 2000, more than two-thirds of Canada's exports were machinery, equipment and other high value-added products. Furthermore, knowledge-based ser-

vices represent one of the fastest-growing areas in our export mix.

Put simply, new-economy industries are powering Canada's strong economic performance. Since 1995 they have expanded at almost four times the rate of the economy as a whole, and they contributed about 40 percent of Canada's growth last year. Clearly, this is good news for Canadians. It is good news for investors as well...

Technology Clusters

Today's Canada is perhaps best illustrated by the emergence of technology clusters – cities and regions that have achieved critical mass and explosive growth in the knowledge economy. These Canadian clusters are anchored by strong research universities and labs, and are host to a whole spectrum of thriving, innovative and entrepreneurial companies – with the people, infrastructure and capital to match. You know about Silicon Valley, Boston, Raleigh-Durham and Dallas. But do you know about the comparable clusters in Montréal, Toronto, Vancouver and Ottawa?"

New World Technologies remanufactures Laser Printer cartridges from across Canada bringing Canadian landfills under much less pressure and contributing to making much more effective use of our limited resources.

Innu-Science sees safeguarding the environment as the key issue in product development, manufacturing biotechnological liquids mixed with non-patholgenic bacteria that have important anti-pollution applications.

The Village of Florenceville in the St. John River Valley of New Brunswick is the international headquarters of McCain Foods Limited, the headquarters of McCain Foods (Canada) and the home of a major McCain manufacturing complex.

The proud staff of the Canadian Light Source, one of the largest single science and technology projects in Canada. The synchrotron is a huge, light generating device housed in a building the size of a football field on the University of Saskatchewan campus. This 'field of beams' will light the way to a new era of innovation for industry and academe.

Art DeFehr, President of Palliser Furniture and employees at one of the company's manufacturing facilities in Winnipeg, Manitoba. Palliser employs people from over 70 nations, including many new Canadians for whom special training is offered.

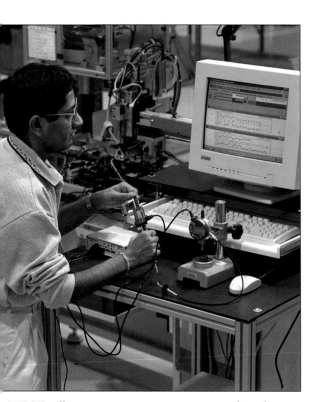

WECO offers over 10,000 custom engineered products – a wide variety of connectors, terminal blocks and electronic modules – to a worldwide customer base.

Railway worker – northern Ontario.

Pratt and Whitney Canada is a world leader in aviation engines powering business and regional aircraft and helicopters. The company also offers advanced engines for industrial applications. Shown here is the PW 500, for the light corporate jet aircraft market.

Stora-Enso-Port Hawkesbury Limited is the largest forest products company and employer in Nova Scotia, playing an active and important role in the communities and forests of the region. Its state of the art supercalendered (SC) paper line at the Port Hawkesbury Mill is located on the Strait of Canso, one of the deepest, ice-free harbours in the World.

Favourable Economic Climate

As Canadians enter into the early years of the new millenium, they can feel very confident as they reflect upon the challenges of the future and the prospects that lie ahead in this new and exciting century.

New economy industries are powering Canada's strong economic performance. Since 1995, these newer industries have expanded at almost four times the rate of the economy as a whole, and they contributed about 40 percent of Canada's growth in 2000.

International trade is critically important to the Canadian economy.

Trade in goods and services represents over 81 percent of the economic output, more than that in any other G7 country. Canada is a geographical and economic crossroads, offering business and trading partners in Europe and Asia access to the world's richest economy.

Under the North American Free Trade Agreement (NAFTA), trade with Canada means trade within the North American market – nearly 400 million people with a combined gross domestic product of more than US $9.4 trillion.

Industry Canada, a federal government department, is helping to make Canadians more productive and competitive in the knowledge-based economy and thus improve the quality of life for Canadians.

Industry Canada is intensifying its efforts on five strategic micro-economic objectives in order to build the competitive advantage that Canada needs for long-term productivity growth.

Trojan Technologies is a Canadian based, high technology environmental company operating internationally. Protecting the Earth's water resources is an environmental necessity, one that Trojan takes seriously in the struggle to make the world a cleaner, healthier place for future generations.

Québec based and owned Canam Steel designs and fabricates specialty structural steel components for the construction industry in Canada, the United States, Mexico, and France.

INDUSTRY IN CANADA

The Honorable Allan Rock is the Minister of Industry.

Industry Canada, a federal government department, is helping to make Canadians more productive and competitive in the knowledge-based economy and thus improve the quality of life for Canadians

Those objectives are: improving Canada's innovation performance; making Canada the most connected nation in the world; building a fair, efficient and competitive marketplace; improving Canada's position as a preferred location for domestic and foreign investment; and working with Canadians to increase Canada's share of global trade.

Canada also enjoys advanced research and development opportunities as well as exceptional research and development incentives. R&D tax treatment is extremely generous – full and immediate write-off for all qualifying direct and indirect current and capital expenditures in R&D. The Government of Canada will at least double its financial commitment to R&D by the year 2010.

Information and Communications Technologies

Canada thrives on innovation. It offers some of the world's most advanced information technologies. Canadian businesses supply leading-edge ICT products and services to stay competitive in a changing world. In the past two years, Canadian ICT firms have invested over $100 billion in expansion and acquisition.

The vibrant Canadian ICT industry has attracted the attention of investors all over the world. Canadian telecommunications companies regularly form strategic alliances with off-shore firms to increase distribution and foster new product development. Canada's enlightened regulatory environment makes it easy for Canadian businesses and their international partners to move innovative new products and services into the global marketplace.

Canadian companies already benefit from one of the world's best communications infrastructures. In addition to a well developed national mesh of public fibre optic and wireless networks, this includes Canada's all-optical advanced research and education network, CA®net3 (at 6000 kilometres, the world's largest fibre optic network). Thus, Canada's high-speed networks open up whole new worlds of economic possibilities. From electronic commerce, multimedia, virtual reality, real-time audio and video – Canadian potential in this industry is unlimited.

Canadian technology clusters generate powerful synergies. Knowledge workers in first-class research facilities produce the new technologies and leading edge ICT solutions of tomorrow. These products and services generate their own entrepreneurial excitement which leads to further innovation and future economic successes.

There are more than 26,000 ICT businesses in Canada with more than 512,000 employees. ICT business include manufacturing of products such as communication equipment, consumer electronics, computer equipment and electronic comp-

Nexen Inc. is a rapidly growing energy and chemicals company with a strong base in western Canada and operations reaching around the globe. The company has a solid commitment to safety, the environment, and social responsibility in its western Canadian operations, Yemen, Colombia, off-shore Australia, Nigeria, and Indonesia.

nents. The industry also includes telecommunications and computer services, software development and wholesale of ICTS.

Research and development by the ICT sector accounted for almost half of total Canadian private sector R&D in 2000 with expenditures of $4.7 billion. The telecommunication equipment industry alone accounted for nearly half of the ICT sectors R&D.

Biotechnology Industry

Biotechnology is experiencing major growth in Canada. The corridor between Montreal and Quebec City, for example, has become the second largest concentration of biopharmaceutical product development in North America. It contains 600 research companies supported by a network of universities and publicly funded research institutions. This growing industry pumps more than $1 billion into the Montreal economy each year, and it invests more than $250 million annually in R&D.

Cities and regions in Canada have achieved critical mass and explosive growth in the knowledge economy. New technologies have permitted regional specializations to flourish, in part because resources are now linked through networks, and the same basic services do not have to be repeated across the country.

The major developed countries have targeted biotechnology as vital for the 21st century. The health sector represents the majority of global activity in biotechnology and accounts for 87 percent of Canadian biotechnology R&D. This emphasis on the health sector will lead to fundamental changes in the areas of diagnosis, treatment and development of drugs.

Biotechnology is an enabling technology that will result in better therapeutic products, higher crop yields, biofuels, healthier foods and a cleaner environment. It will impact on almost

Cranberries being harvested at Port Carling, Ontario.

everything that affects the quality of peoples' lives. Biotechnology promises well-paid knowledge-based jobs. This means that highly educated Canadians will find it easier to connect with exciting research opportunities here at home.

Canada is number two, after the United States, in the world in terms of the number of firms devoting more than half their revenues to R&D. In 1999, there were 361 biotechnology companies in Canada, $1.9 billion in revenues, $413 million in exports and $832 million in R&D. These companies are primarily small and medium-sized, and in 1997 accounted for 11,723 well-paid jobs.

Genome Canada

International experts agree that genomics is the key to the future of biotechnology. Genome Canada is spear-heading a national effort to

make Canada a world leader in genomics research, accelerating our investment in new areas of ground breaking research. Genome Canada is a not-for-profit, national partnership-based scientific enterprise.

The Government of Canada has committed $300 million in funding for Genome Canada that is expected to lever a similar commitment from provincial governments and other partners.

Automotive Industry

Canada's automotive industry produces light-duty vehicles including cars, vans, sport utility vehicles and pickup trucks, heavy duty vehicles, including trucks, transit buses, school buses, intercity buses and military vehicles, and a wide range of parts and systems used in such vehicles.

The Canadian automotive industry is part of the fully integrated North American automotive industry and has the benefit of favourable access to North American markets through the North American Free Trade Agreement. Canada's automotive sector ranked as the fourth largest in the world in 1999, behind the United States, Japan and Germany. The sector was a major contributor to the Canadian economy, accounting for 15% of manufacturing GDP, and 7% of manufacturing employment in 1999.

Canada has also developed world class vehicle systems and parts manufacturing industries. The scale and output of the automotive sector benefits a number of Canadian supplier industries. In the primary metals sector, it is estimated that the automotive sector purchases 37% of domestic iron production, 20% of steel production, and 14% of processed aluminum production. In addition, the sector purchases 17% of Canada's rubber production, 15% of its machine shop production, 13% of its wire goods and 8% of its glass products.

Aerospace Industry

The aerospace industry is one of the strongest pillars in the new Canadian knowledge-based economy. Canadian aerospace firms produce world class products, such as aircraft, parts, space

communications and electronic systems for the global aerospace market.

Many aerospace firms provide maintenance and repair services for clients around the world. Unlike the aerospace industry in the United States, Canada's aerospace sector is primarily engaged in civilian products and services.

On the world stage, the Canadian aerospace industry ranks as the sixth largest in the world and the global leader in many product categories.

Within Canada, the aerospace industry accounts for 3.1 percent of manufacturing GDP. Over 700 establishments, located in all parts of the country, comprise the manufacturing base for the industry, the bulk of which can be found in aerospace industry clusters around Montreal and Toronto.

In 1999, the Canadian aerospace firms had sales of $19.6 billion. Sales growth has been robust in the past 10 years, especially in the aircraft and parts sector where shipments have increased 142 percent since 1990.

The industry employs an estimated 92,000 Canadians and, in recent years, has been a strong source of new jobs for high skilled, knowledge workers.

In the overall industry, 18 percent of Canada's aerospace workforce are

engineers. This highly skilled workforce provides the backbone for the significant research, development and innovation capabilities in this industry. Canada's aerospace industry is highly export oriented, producing for the global marketplace rather than the relatively small domestic market. Over 70 percent of the Canadian aerospace industry's sales are derived from exports.

Small and Medium-Sized Businesses

Small and medium-sized businesses have been major players in the development of Canadian innovation and in Canada's economic growth. There are about two million of these dynamic enterprises in Canada.

They have contributed to a reduction in the unemployment rate, approaching its lowest level in 24 years. Some 380,000 new jobs were created in 2000 and strong economic growth is expected to continue in this sector of the economy.

Summary

The spread and impact of technological change will continue to drive economic growth in all industry sectors in Canada. The power of the new economy is in its long term ability to promote enduring change, to add momentum to a wide range of existing industries, and to give rise to whole new fields of industrial and scientific enterprise.

Canada began its first century by building a railroad to conquer its vast distances. Canada is beginning the 21st century leading in technologies that will abolish distance entirely, creating new national networks of cooperating communities, interests and enterprises linked together instantaneously.

Innovation is key to success in this new economy, and Canadian industries are well positioned to continue to succeed.

Air Nunavut.

Simulation and Beyond

Headquartered in Canada and employing approximately 7,000 people, CAE is the world's leading supplier of commercial full flight simulators with over 80% of the global market.

In 2001, Acadian Seaplants Limited in Nova Scotia introduced the first ever edible yellow seaweed into the Asian marketplace.

Canadian Pacific Railway. These ribbons of steel were once the primary link between the Atlantic and Pacific.

Canada in Space

Dr. Marc Garneau, seen here in the official STS-97 pre-launch picture, is one of the most respected figures in Canada, a leading space nation. Canada's first astronaut to go into space, Dr. Garneau participated in three missions before being appointed President of the Canadian Space Agency.

The Canadian space sector is internationally competitive, export-oriented, and at the leading edge of the shift of Canada's economy from natural resources to information and high technology.

The Canadian space industry, composed of some 250 firms and organisms from across Canada, employs over 5,500 people. Some 45% of $1.2 billion annual revenues are from exports – the highest percentage in the world.

Scientific discovery and the development of innovative, leap-frog technologies being pursued under the Canadian Space Program will help promote a more competitive space industry, and create new job opportunities for Canadians from coast to coast.

Incredibly, for all the accomplishments along the way, the journey into space has not yet spanned a human lifetime. Only 44 years ago, a small Russian aluminum sphere called Sputnik orbited the earth for three months and in doing so launched the Space Age.

Today, 15 nations, including Canada, are in the midst of the most ambitious multinational science and engineering project of our time – the construction of an International Space Station. (Canadian Space Agency)

The Canadarm.

The red-coloured Canada logo is stamped on the Canadarm's white protective blanket, as seen by the astronauts in this picture taken during a space shuttle mission.

NATURAL RESOURCES

The Honorable Herb Dhaliwal is the Minister of Natural Resources.

Canada's goal is to become and remain one of the world's smartest stewards, developers, users and exporters of its energy resources – high-tech, environmentally friendly, socially responsible, productive and competitive – a living model of sustainable development.

Offshore Technology –
Hibernia Oil and Gas field project,
Jeanne d'Arc Basin, Newfoundland.

Canada is a world leader in advanced hydrogen fuel-cell technologies.
(Photo courtesy of Ford Canada)

District energy heating systems are operating in the Ontario Aboriginal community of
Grassy Narrows; the Québec Community of Oujé-Bougoumou (shown here), whose
system received a United Nations award for sustainable communities; and in the
cities of Sudbury and Windsor (Ontario) and Charlottetown, Prince Edward Island.

Energy to Innovate, Power to Serve: Canadian Technology and Know-How in the Energy Sector

Energy in Canada

Canada depends on the richness of its energy resources and the industries they support. Canadians are very aware that they must address today's energy needs without compromising either the environment or the ability of future generations to meet their energy needs.

Natural Resources Canada

In the Government of Canada, Natural Resources Canada (NRCan) is the department responsible for energy. This department plays a pivotal role in helping shape the enormous economic, social and environmental contributions of the natural resources sector to the quality of life for Canadians.

Visit www.nrcan.gc.ca to learn more about NRCan and Canada's natural resources.

Sustainable Development

Through partnership and innovation, Natural Resources Canada works with Canadians in all sectors to make wise use of their resources, including energy. Economic, environmental and social factors are balanced in decisions about energy use and resource development.

Canada is a world leader in the sustainable development of energy. It uses innovative technologies and expertise in the production and use of all types of energy.

The new frontiers of Canada's energy industry – the North, and the marine environment of offshore eastern Canada – require unique approaches to minimize the detrimental effects of resource extraction, while seeking new ways to carry out development that preserves the environment.

Climate change

A particular challenge to sustainable development is climate change. As a northern nation, Canada is especially susceptible to a changing climate.

The Government of Canada is committed to taking action to reduce greenhouse gas emissions that contribute to climate change. Together with 160 other countries, we are working through the Kyoto Protocol to address this global challenge.

Canada is reducing emissions while balancing economic, environmental and social concerns through good management, balanced fair measures and strategic investments in innovative technologies.

Use of Energy

Sustainable energy development is vitally important to Canada because energy is essential to running its economy, bridging the vast distances of its rugged terrain, and, more basically, keeping its citizens warm in the winter and cool in the summer.

Canada's growing economy and growing population are creating a higher demand for energy.

The energy sector is a cornerstone of the Canadian economy. In addition, energy intensive activities, such as natural resources extraction and processing, are an important feature of the economy.

600 kw wind turbine at Belly River, Alberta.
(Photo courtesy of Vision Quest Windelectric Inc.)

Energy Resources

Canada is fortunate to have abundant energy resources – crude oil, natural gas, uranium and coal, and renewable energy sources such as water and biomass. (agricultural and forestry residue)

All sources are being developed and used to achieve a clean, efficient energy supply. The diversification of energy sources ensures Canadians a secure and reliable supply of energy.

Renewable and Alternative Energy

Canada is a world leader in the production of renewable energy: 17 percent of its primary energy supply comes from renewable sources.

Canada's renewable energy production comes mostly from water (hydroelectricity) and wood. Other emerging sources include solar, wind, earth and other sources of biomass such as agricultural products.

Alternative energy sources include fuel cells and transportation fuels such as natural gas, ethanol and propane.

Use of renewable and alternative energy makes a growing contribution to satisfying Canada's energy needs in ways that are economical and environmentally sensitive.

Electricity

Canada is the fifth largest producer of electric power in the world, generating four percent of the world's total. It is the second-largest producer of hydroelectric power. Canadian industry has the capabilities needed to develop electric power throughout the world. Products range from small-hydro installations through efficient modular gas turbines to the world's largest air-cooled hydro generator in Venezuela.

In the nuclear field, the CANDU™ reactor system, developed in Canada, is safely and reliably providing electricity on four continents.

Oil and Gas

Canada is the third largest producer of natural gas and the eleventh largest producer of crude oil in the world. Its oil sands and heavy oil represent one-third of the world's known useful petroleum reserves.

Canada has huge undeveloped energy resources for future development, including major crude oil and natural gas deposits in offshore areas and massive reserves of oil sands (bituminous) in Alberta.

Dam and reservoir.

Canada's expertise in the oil and gas field is extensive. The Canadian oil and gas industry has led the way in developing and providing equipment and techniques capable of operating anywhere in the world, including continental shelves. Canada has developed some of the largest and most efficient oil and gas operations in the world.

Energy Research and Development

Efficient technologies are needed to extract, process and transport energy resources in a sustainable manner. Canadians have placed an emphasis on developing and using the best technologies available.

Canada's research and development focusses on the next generation of climate friendly technologies. Activities encompass everything from advanced hydrocarbon technologies and energy efficient technologies for homes, communities and industry, to alternative transportation fuels, renewable energy sources and emerging technologies such as fuel cells.

Examples of leading-edge Canadian technologies:

- advanced commercial buildings and homes that use one third less energy compared to current construction;
- Solarwalls™ for preheating air for large buildings;
- RETScreen™, an advanced software and simulation tool for renewable energy technologies;
- CANDU™ nuclear reactors;
- vehicles and power generation plants powered by fuel cells; and
- carbon dioxide capture and storage.

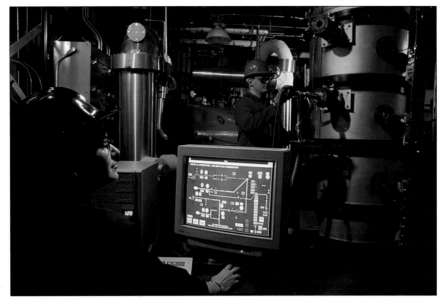

Natural Resources Canada researchers developing advanced carbon dioxide capture and storage technologies.

Making use of photovoltaic technology in Canada's North.

Canada's R-2000 homes are energy-efficient, offer superior indoor air quality and use environmentally responsible products.

The Sudbury Basin contains one of the world's largest deposits of nickel and copper and the famous Sudbury nickel (Canada's five cent coin) is the striking landmark of a region rich in deposits of nickel sulphide ore, as well as lead, zinc, silver and other metals.

Diamonds from the Northwest Territories are becoming recognized and sought after for their exceptional clarity and brilliance, and, are creating employment and new careers for aboriginal residents.

The Men of the Deeps keep the memory of Canada's coal mining traditions alive through their wonderful music.

Area of Canada covered by forested land: 417.6 million hectares.

Canada's share of the world's forests by area: 10%
Share of the world's boreal forest: 35%
Tree species in Canada: 180
Canada's global ranking in the export of forest products:1
Ranking of Canada in world newsprint production: 1

Canadian Geographic, Eco-Audit, May/June 1999.

Halliburton Forest.

Herring weir seining Grand Manon Island, New Brunswick.

Roughly 7 million Canadians live in coastal areas where many people in smaller communities depend on the ocean's resources and tourism to make a living.

- There were 24,200 commercial fishing vessels in 1999.
- The value of Canada's marine fisheries landings in 1999 reached a record high of $1.92 billion, up 18% from 1998.
- Canada's fishery exports (506,312 tonnes) were valued at $3.7 billion in 1999, up 11% from 1998.
- Canada's fishery imports were $2 billion in 1999, leaving a trade surplus of $1.7 billion.
- Aquaculture is one of the fastest-growing food production activities in the world. In 1999, the Canadian aquaculture industry produced approximately 113,083 tonnes of product, which represents 22.5% of the value of Canadian fish and seafood production. (Fisheries and Oceans, Canada)

CANADA'S PROVINCES
AND TERRITORIES

Newfoundland

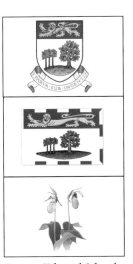

Prince Edward Island

Nova Scotia

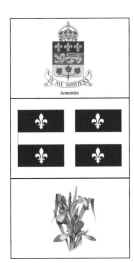

New Brunswick

Québec

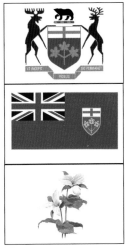

Ontario

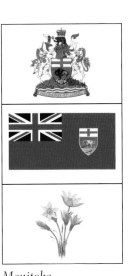

Manitoba

Saskatchewan

Alberta

Editors Note:
Canada has ten provinces and three territories with their own distinctive symbols. In the section that follows, we will transit this vast country from East to West, starting with the easternmost Atlantic province of Newfoundland (which is closer to Ireland than to the Canadian province of Ontario) and culminating on the Pacific coast. For the aerial traveller, traversing Canada is the equivalent of spanning the Atlantic plus the entire width of Europe.

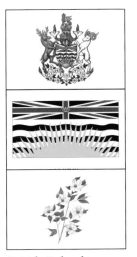

British Columbia

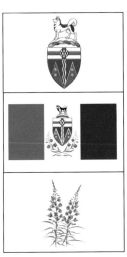

Yukon

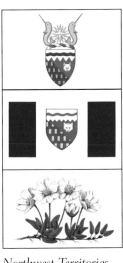

Northwest Territories

Nunavut

'This place of pine-clad hills, this smiling land as loved our fathers so we love – their prayer we raise to heaven above – God guard thee, Newfoundland. (Ode to Newfoundland)

NEWFOUNDLAND LABRADOR

"Beneath the lenticular clouds a slice of the Earth's mantle sits peacefully alongside Trout River Pond. The Tablelands in Gros Morne National Park was pushed up from deep below an ancient ocean by a continental collision about 450 million years ago, and is one of the reasons that the park is an UNESCO World Heritage Site." (Roberta Bondar)

Glynmill Inn, Corner Brook.

Ruth Canning is Chair of the Heritage Foundation of Newfoundland and Labrador

Winterholme, St. John's.

The cultural landscape of a people tells the story of lessons learned from the past, of adaptations to the natural environment, and of lifestyles, aesthetic expression and social values. It is, therefore, the essence of community fabric and pride. Newfoundland and Labrador has a distinctive architecture because it has a history and an economy that is quite different from that of most North Atlantic nations. While we have considerable land based resources, we are fundamentally a sea-born people with a culture shaped largely by the sea.

Newfoundland is the only place that, having started life as a fishing nation, has remained one until the present day. This continuity has had a marked influence on our architecture and on our cultural landscape.

The need for a place to make fish, to dry those fish and to shelter the fishers during the season produced characteristic building types and the use of particular structural forms which, once common around the Atlantic rim, can now only be found in Newfoundland and Labrador. The stage and the flake, while they are not

Newfoundland creations, are the most representative of our building types. Less visible, but equally distinctive, is our use of full-studded construction in which walls are made not of frame but of rough cut logs set vertically. Used commonly for tilts and other temporary accommodation, it was converted into a structural system for permanent houses and was used through the Great Depression.

As nineteenth-century photographs show, Newfoundland's cultural landscape is unmistakably different from that of its North American neighbours. The relationship between the fisheries buildings and the houses, lodges and churches of the outport is very close, all gathered about the water's edge; the church and lodge on a height above, the houses adjacent to the stages and very frequently surrounded by flakes. The houses themselves tended to be very simple: a succession of steeply-pitched roofs over wooden-clapboard walls, bare of decoration until the end of the century. This simplicity was even to be found in the merchant's house and extended to the larger towns. It was in the churches that the people, led generally by their priest or minister, expressed their architectural ambitions.

It is not just the grand old houses that make Newfoundland and Labrador the place that it is. It is the ordinary houses, the wharf, and the plant, and the views of the cold North

The humpback whale breaches for the cameras. 22 species of whales feed in the rich ocean currents off Newfoundland and Labrador.

Atlantic. Many communities retain a strong sense of the past in their houses and outbuildings, their street patterns, their fences and their gardens.

The most important of our heritage is the people - the ones here now, as much as those who were here before. Our cultural heritage includes local songs and stories, paths and parks, means of travel, folklore, traditional crafts and occupations. It is this authentic sense of place, expressed through our buildings, landscape and other heritage resources, that visitors seek out to celebrate and share in.

What is also distinctive is that so much of this cultural landscape has remained comparatively intact through the present century. But more of this remarkable heritage is being lost with each passing year. More of it is threatened but much of it can be saved, and much has already been saved as a consequence of the activities of the Heritage Foundation of Newfoundland and Labrador.

The Heritage Foundation of Newfoundland and Labrador is a non-profit organization which was established by the provincial Government of Newfoundland and Labrador in 1984 to stimulate an understanding of and an appreciation for the architectural heritage of the province.

The Foundation, an invaluable source of information for historic restoration, supports and contributes to the preservation and restoration of buildings of architectural or historical significance. The Heritage Foundation designates buildings and other structures as Registered Heritage Structures and may provide grants for the purpose of preservation and/or restoration of such structures.

One area where the Foundation has had great success is in the overlap between our heritage and the cultural sector. The growing interest in cultural and heritage tourism has seen such a tremendous growth in the establishment of bed and breakfasts throughout the Province. Without a doubt the most popular of these are in Registered Heritage Structures where the Buildings have retained their original architectural features. Examples include Campbell House and Gover House in Trinity, Silver Linings in Bonavista, The Thorndyke in Grand Bank, Winterholme, The Lea and Waterford Manor in St. John's, Glynmill Inn in Corner Brook, Pinehurst and Keneally Manor in Carbonear, Adams' House in Cape onion, and Hampshire Cottage in Harbour Grace. It is successes like these that make the business of preserving, promoting, and protecting the heritage of Newfoundland and Labrador worthwhile.

It was on the historic, wind-swept site of Signal Hill that Guglielmo Marconi received the first transatlantic wireless message one century ago on December 1, 1901. Newfoundlanders and visitors around the world recently celebrated this achievement which introduced the information age.

History

Newfoundland's earliest indigenous people were the Beothuk Indians who inhabited the Island for several thousand years before European colonization. Tragically, by the early 1800s, disease and conflicts with settlers led to their extinction. There were, and still are, a relatively large number of Inuit concentrated in the coastal communities of Northern Labrador.

The earliest indication of European settlement in North America is the Norse site located at L'Anse aux Meadows on the tip of Newfoundland's Great Northern Peninsula. Radiocarbon dating suggests that the Norse settled there only for a short time, between 990 and 1050 A.D, five hundred years before Columbus.

In 1497, the Genoese navigator Giovanni Caboto, known as John Cabot, became the first recorded European to spot mainland Canada, when he sailed along the shorelines of what are now Newfoundland, Labrador, and Nova Scotia.

He, like many of the explorers of the time were searching for a Passage to Asia which would lead to the wealth of China and the East Indies. Cabot's excited seamen spread word of the fabulous riches of the western ocean, a place 'where the sea is swarming with fish which can be taken not only with the net, but in baskets let down by a stone so that it sinks in the water.'

Baby seal.

John Cabot landed on the island on June 24, 1497, the feast of St. John the Baptist, claiming it for his patron, Henry V11 of England. In 1583, Sir Humphrey Gilbert sailed an English flotilla into the naturally sheltered harbour at St. John's claiming the area for Queen Elizabeth I.

Subsequently, Anglo-French warfare shaped the history of Newfoundland during the 17th and 18th centuries. With the signing of the Treaty of Paris in 1763, Britain's hard won sovereignty over Newfoundland and the fishing banks was finally recognized.

Newfoundland received responsible government in 1855, but it was not until 1949, after three hard fought referenda, that the colony became the 10th province in the Canadian Federation.

St. John's is the oldest settlement in the western world. With its population of over 100,000, the colorful capital of Newfoundland and Labrador is now an active centre for investment and business activity in offshore oil development. Hibernia, Terra Nova and other oil field developments promise an exciting future for this proud, daring, and resilient people.

L'Anse aux Meadows.

Bay de Verde Fishing Village, Gros Morne National Park.

Gros Morne National Park, Newfoundland.

The towers of ice off the coast of Newfoundland always captivate visitors. (Iceberg off Trinity Bay).

The population of Newfoundland and Labrador came mostly from the southwest of England and the south and southeast of Ireland.

The early migration to the island was linked to the fishery and much of the population was spread widely around a rugged coastline in small outport settlements. Many of these tiny enclaves were a long distance from larger centres of population and cut off for lengthy periods by winter ice or bad weather.

The isolated conditions, along with the distinctive culture of the immigrants to Newfoundland produced an incredible treasure chest of local customs, stories, songs and legends, as well as idioms and dialects, which delight, charm, and intrigue the visitor.

Salvage Cove.

"The Fairest Land 'tis Possible to See."
(Jacques Cartier)

Lighthouse at Tyron Head, Prince Edward Island.

PRINCE EDWARD ISLAND

Gilbert Ralph Clements is the former Lieutenant Governor of Prince Edward Island.

"The fairest land 'tis possible to see," were the words Jacques Cartier used to describe Prince Edward Island when he discovered, it in 1534. And since that discovery almost five hundred years ago, visitors to our Island agree with the words of the French explorer and continue to marvel at its beauty and tranquility.

Prince Edward Islanders are truly a distinct breed of people. We refer to our province as 'the Island' as if there were no other. And indeed we all feel that it is one of a kind, a special place, a place we are proud to call home. Islanders are noted for their hospitality and visitors are treated to our famous 'down-East hospitality'. A warm welcome awaits visitors and tourists alike.

Another group of famous people to land on Prince Edward Island arrived in 1864. They landed at Charlottetown Harbour and walked up Great George Street to a meeting place where they laid the basis for the beginnings of this great country. The Fathers of Confederation met right here in Charlottetown, and they 'builded better than they knew'; their deliberations led to the Canadian union and the birth of this great country, Canada. In fact, when these forefathers met in Charlottetown, they posed on the front steps of Fanningbank, the official residence of the Lieutenant Governor, for a portrait that has since become famous.

Do you remember the antics of that little red head, Anne of Green Gables? It was right here on Prince Edward Island that Lucy Maud Montgomery penned the stories that made places like 'Lovers Lane,' and the 'Lake of Shining Waters' famous. You can visit Green Gables house yourself or attend a live performance of 'Anne' at Confederation Centre of the Arts where the show has played to sold-out audiences for the past thirty-six years. I guarantee you will fall in love with kindred spirits, Anne and Diana, and other members of the musical cast.

Because PEI is my home province, I have a great appreciation for our Island. Our way of life is like no other; we keep abreast of the latest in technology and yet we live a simple life. In March of 1997, PEI made history by becoming the first and only Canadian jurisdiction to provide the entire province with access to a high-speed network which can carry data, audio,graphics, and video 5,500 times faster than the current industry norm. As a result, PEI is the first province to have Internet access in every school and public library. And the information revolution has meant that Prince Edward Island businesses, in partnership with provincial and federal governments are on the way to transforming Canada's smallest province into one of its smartest!

In the spring of 1997 we saw the opening of the Confederation Bridge, linking the Island to the rest of Canada. This structure is touted as the longest multi span bridge over ice covered water in the world. Still, locals and visitors alike continue to enjoy our relaxed style of living. We are content and comfortable here on PEI with time for a friendly hello and amicable chatter. This pattern of life suits us well and appeals not only to locals but also to those who find the hustle and bustle of big city life just a little too hectic.

As you read through the section on our province I hope you see for yourself why the province is unique. May I extend a warm invitation to you to come to our Island, and experience for yourself our warmth and charm. Walk on our miles of sandy beaches, sample our delicious seafood and view our rolling countryside. You won't be disappointed!

Anne of Green Gables.

Lobsters.

The 'garden province,' as it is justifiably known, is famous for the rainbow of beaches which fringe the Island. The visitor can find red, champagne, and pink hues all along the shoreline.

Prince Edward Island's trademark rich, red soil and lush, rolling farmland translate into an excellent location for mixed farming. The Island produces one-third of the total volume of tablestock potatoes in Canada; names like Russet Burbank, Superior, and Yukon gold are known world-wide!

Fishing and aquaculture are of great importance to the Island's economy, and generate, in total, in excess of $250 million annually.

The riches of the sea translate into some of the finest cuisine in Canada. Lobster, Island blue mussels, Malpeque oysters – all kinds of juicy gastronomical delights – await the golfer, the hiker, the history lover, the Anne of Green Gables affectionado, the theatre goer; as well as those who come to take in 'a bit of the tune' – the beach hugger, the beach bird watcher, and the sailer home from the sea.

Woodleigh Replicas.

PEI is now a world class golf destination!

Fishing Village.

Province House, Charlottetown.

History

The province's name was adopted in 1799 to honour Prince Edward, Duke of Kent, fourth son of King George 111, who was then commander-in-chief of British North America and was stationed in Halifax when the island was named. The prince was Queen Victoria's father.

Aboriginal peoples called Prince Edward island "Abegweit," derived from a Mi'kmaq word loosely translated as "cradled in the waves." Early French settlers called it Ile Ste Jean: when the Treaty of Paris in 1763 gave the island to the British, the name was translated to St. John's Island. Prince Edward Island has also had a number of nicknames including the "Million Acre-Farm" and "The Garden of the Gulf."

Although the Mi'kmaq Indians have inhabited the island for the last 2,000 years, there are indications that their ancestors lived there as long as l0,000 years ago. These aboriginal peoples are said to have reached the island by crossing the low plain now covered by the Northumberland Strait.

The Island was visited intermittently by French fishermen in the 17th century, but Europeans did not settle permanently on the Island until the second decade of the 18th century.

Prince Edward Island hosted the first of the confederation conferences at Charlottetown in 1864. However, the island's leaders dropped out of the confederation discussions after the Quebec City conference later in the same year because they feared their autonomy would be jeopardized by joining a large Canadian union.

Less than ten years later, that decision was reversed. The debt incurred in building a railway for the island, pressure from the British government, and the attractive promises of the Canadian government compelled Prince Edward Island to join Confederation in 1873. The Canadian promises included an absorption of the debt, year-round communication with the mainland and funds to buy out the absentee landowners.

Prince Edward Island is known as the birthplace of Confederation; the gentle island where the national dream was conceived. Province House National Historic Site, called the Colonial House when it opened in 1847, was the site of the talks leading to Confederation in 1867. It is the current seat of the Prince Edward Island government, and, for history lovers, a very popular spot indeed.

Sir John A. Macdonald Room.

Tuna Fishing.

The Confederation Bridge is the longest bridge over ice-covered waters in the world. It's construction is viewed as one of the most significant Canadian engineering events of the 20th century. The highest point of the bridge is the shipping navigation span which is 60 metres. Construction began in October, 1993 and the bridge opened to traffic on May 31, 1997.

A child of the Island wanders through a field of wild lupins.

The joy of this young man celebrating sunset over the Atlantic coast can only be imagined.

O Canada!

Our home and native land!
True patriot love
in all thy sons command
With glowing hearts
we see thee rise
The True North
strong and Free!
From far and wide,
O Canada
We stand on guard
for thee.
God keep our land
glorious and free!
O Canada
we stand on guard for thee
O Canada
we stand on guard for thee.

O Canada!

Terre de nos aïeux
Ton front est ceint
de fleurons glorieux!
Car ton bras
sait porter l'èpée,
Il sait porter
la croix!
Ton histoire
est une épopée
Des plus
brillants exploits
Et ta valeur
de foi trempée
Prótegera nos foyers
et nos droits
Prótegera nos foyers
et nos droits.

"Ciad Mile Failte –
A Hundred Thousand Welcomes,"
To Canada's Ocean Playground.

The billowing sails of Nova Scotia's Bluenose II symbolize rich history and the adventuresome spirit of this proud Atlantic province.

NOVA SCOTIA

Like many proud Nova Scotians, I am always delighted to share my deep love of this beautiful province with colleagues, friends and visitors from all parts of the globe.

In this wonderful world by the sea, one is never more than thirty minutes from the sandy beaches, vast tidal flats and majestic vistas which characterize our breathtaking shoreline. In fact, if you look carefully at a map of the province, you will see that the sea virtually surrounds our province and its 920,000 residents. It is not surprising that Nova Scotia, as the most easterly point on the North American mainland, has been for centuries, the first stop for many vessels coming from Europe.

I have explored nearly every square inch of Nova Scotia and have never failed to find something new in my travels. I always take great pleasure in watching the dramatic rise and fall of the highest tides in the world at the Bay of Fundy, and exploring the historic Evangeline Trail which parallels the Fundy coast. This scenic route traverses some of North America's earliest European history, as well as the delightful villages and orchards of the Annapolis Valley.

My family and I have always loved the romantic Sunrise Trail which winds through gently rolling farmlands and a stunning tapestry of emerald green fields that meet the sparkling blue waters of the Northumberland Strait. A special treat in this region has always been the world-famous Highland Games in Antigonish, where visitors and locals alike are swept away in the captivating music of bagpipes and fiddles and traditional Celtic dance.

The magic of Cape Breton Island and the splendor of the Cabot Trail's bold highlands are legendary. Cape Breton's most famous resident, Alexander Graham Bell, once said, "I have travelled around the globe. I have seen the Canadian and the American Rockies, the Andes and the Highlands of Scotland, but for simple beauty, Cape Breton outrivals them all." Bell fell in love with the region and built his beautiful estate, Beinn Bhreagh, on the shores of the spectacular Bras d'Or Lakes, where he lived and worked for the rest of his life.

Nova Scotia's coat of arms, granted in 1625, is by far the oldest of any province or territory in Canada. At nearly every fork in the road, the visitor encounters colourful chapters in the history of the province and the country at large.

I think of Halifax's famous hilltop fort at the Citadel National Historic Site and of Nova Scotia's thrilling International Tattoo; of the Grand Pré National Historic Site, the Cape Breton Miners' Museum, and Halifax's Maritime Museum of the Atlantic, home to the permanent exhibit, 'Titanic'. (It must be remembered that the task of recovering bodies from the ill fated vessel fell to a number of Canadian ships dispatched from Halifax. Many were buried in three Halifax cemeteries.)

We often bring visitors to stroll through the historic homes, stores, and workshops of centuries past, beautifully reenacted at Fortress Louisbourg. No one I have ever

Honorable Myra A. Freeman is the Lieutenant Governor of Nova Scotia

known has ceased to marvel at the living testimony of our past so faithfully recorded at Port Royal, the site of Samuel de Champlain's original fort built in 1605. Of special significance are the poignant memories movingly recreated at the National Historic Site of Pier 21, the Gateway to Canada for generations of immigrants, wartime refugees, troops, warbrides and their young children; and a place many Nova Scotians feel to be the real Soul of Canada.

Yes, whether it is the world heritage town of Lunenburg, or the sight of the regal sails of the The Bluenose II entering one of the world's finest harbours at Halifax, whether it is the sweetness of apple blossom time in the Annapolis Valley, or the haunting presence of the famous lighthouse at Peggy's Cove, it goes without saying that this jewel of a province is God's paradise on earth.

As an educator, I have often reflected on the great good fortune we have as Nova Scotians to live and work and raise families in a place where the caring and sharing of our people is one of our strongest natural resources. Community spirit is still the essence of who we are, and remains so, even as members of our highly educated workforce take to information technology and the new knowledge economy like fish to water.

We have the highest number of post-secondary students per capita in North America and the most universities per capita in Canada. It is small wonder that our talented Netizens of the 21st century are, like the shipbuilders and the sailors of the 19th, able to live anywhere and succeed everywhere.

And now, as millions of acres of our ocean floor have been opened up to oil and gas exploration and development (with the potential existing for more than half a dozen Sable gas projects and the extraordinary possibilities in the Laurentian sub-basin), the future of Nova Scotia appears very bright indeed. I believe we live in the best province in the greatest country in the world. And you can rest assured that the teacher in me has made me a keen observer.

The Halifax harbour front is an enchanting mix of 18th and 19th century architecture along with modern glass and steel skyscrapers.

History

The Mi'kmaq nation of the Algonquian linguistic group inhabited Nova Scotia long before the arrival of European explorers. They allied with the French throughout early Canadian history. Fur trader Pierre de Monts and the French explorer Samuel de Champlain established the first agricultural settlement in Port Royal (now Annapolis Royal, Nova Scotia). It was here that the oldest social group in North America, the Order of Good Cheer, was formed.

The Mi'kmaq alliance proved invaluable to the French in the century long struggle against Britain for control over the region. At the time, Nova Scotia, parts of Quebec, New Brunswick and Maine were known as Acadia. By 1713, the region would fall to the British, except for Ile Royale. (now known as Cape Breton) The British would go on to the capture the mighty fortress of Louisbourg located on the island, but in a reversal of fortune, it would be returned to the French in 1748.

Partly to compensate for the return of Louisbourg, Great Britain began a full scale effort to establish its control of mainland Nova Scotia. The city of Halifax was founded in 1749, and by the end of the 1750's would become Britain's key military base on the North Atlantic seaboard of America. In response to the rise of Halifax, the French posted larger garrisons to Louisbourg.

For a century the Acadians (French speaking settlers in the Minas Basin

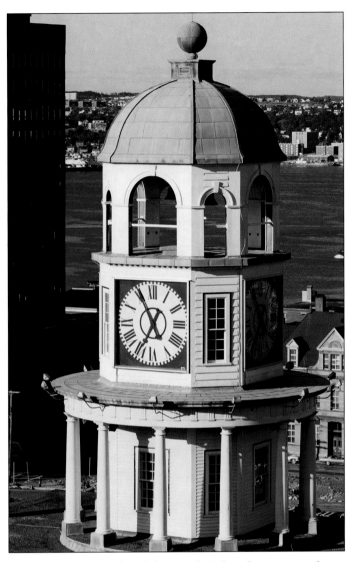

A magnificent reminder of the British Colonial presence is the Halifax Citadel National Historic site.

area) had been able to remain a neutral enclave within British territory. They had occupied the best land of the colony for generations, lands that they had reclaimed from the Fundy tides. In the dangerous atmosphere of the period, British distrust of the Acadians mounted. Powerless and unoffending, they were completely unprepared for the British deportation order of 1755 which led to their expulsion from their ancestral lands and subsequent displacement in alien societies. 'Le grand dérangement' was a tragic event which was immortalized in the poem 'Evangeline' by Longfellow.

By the early 19th century, some of the Acadians returned, but as new set-

tlers had occupied their old diked lands, the centre of Acadian society shifted to the province of New Brunswick. In the meantime, German settlements took root in the Lunenburg area of the south shore of Nova Scotia, while Ulstermen from Northern Ireland came to the Truro area. The Scots favoured the highlands of Cape Breton and Pictou, along the shores of the Northumberland Strait. Many French settlers also settled in Cape Breton while Yorkshiremen went to the west of the province.

In 1848, largely through the efforts of journalist and politician Joseph Howe, Nova Scotia became the first British colony to win responsible government.

Nova Scotia and three other provinces joined the federation called the Dominion of Canada in 1867. At the time the province was a leader in international shipbuilding and in the lumber and fish trades.

Town Crier, Historic Properties, Halifax.

Louisbourg, on Cape Breton Island, is the largest historical reconstruction in North America of French colonial life and times.

Alexander Graham Bell, the inventor of the telephone, fell in love with Baddeck and built his beautiful home on nearby Beinn Bhreagh. It was from Baddeck that Bell's Silver Dart recorded the first airplane flight in the British Empire in February, 1909.

Annapolis county farmer.

The Evangeline Trail begins at historic Yarmouth, a famous seaport intimately linked with Maine and Massachusetts in the USA. The Trail curves in through sweetly perfumed orchards and bumper pumpkin crops in the Annapolis Valley. Evangeline was the heroine of Longfellow's moving poem about the deportation of the Acadians from Grand Pré.

Apple orchard.

Grand Pré.

The Cabot Trail, Cape Breton – soaring eagles, pods of whales, gentle pastoral serenity and ancient cliffs make this one of the world's most sought after scenic drives.

A lone piper's Celtic soliloquy.

"A Place of Sheer Beauty
Where Adventuresome People Have created a Crucible
In Bold Social Initiatives."

(Louis Robichaud)

The Bay of Fundy's awe-inspiring high tides take the breath away! It is a vast natural treasure house of the sea where one can find an abundance of sandstone sea caves and marine life of all description, and of course the gigantic flower pot collection better known as the spectacular Hopewell Rocks.

At low tide on the Hopewell Rocks, one can walk the ocean floor... and at high tide, when the wild waves rise to the heights of office buildings, the daring kayakers do their thing!

NEW BRUNSWICK

N'étant ni historien, ni poète, alors que la tâche exigerait, sans doute, une alliance de ces deux vocations, j'ai témérairement accepté, néanmoins, de présenter au lecteur ma province natale où, d'ailleurs, je viens de me réinstaller à demeure.

Ce serait motif suffisant pour parler d'abondance du riche patrimoine historique du Nouveau-Brunswick, de ses ressources, de ses résidants et de la place que la province occupe dans la fédération canadienne. Après tout, c'est un truisme que de dire qu'on ne parle bien que de ce qu'on aime.

Mais alors surgirait la tentation des clichés faciles qui, même véridiques, n'en sont pas moins éculés. Mieux vaut laisser au texte et aux photographies qui suivent le soin d'une découverte aussi complète que soignée.

Une simple question s'impose: qu'est-ce qui distingue le Nouveau-Brunswick des autres provinces et territoires du Canada? Paradoxalement, la réponse est à la fois facile et

complexe. Ce sont bien sûr, ses citoyens et citoyennes autant que sa géographie particulière.

Certes, les citoyens et les citoyennes du Nouveau-Brunswick partagent les mêmes vertus civiques que l'on trouve dans toutes les sociétiés. Prétendre à l'exclusivité relèverait du vulgaire chauvinisme. Cependant, le développement de la province est le résultat de tant d'apports disparates que le Nouveau-Brunswick a acquis un caractère qui lui est propre, sinon unique en son genre.

Simple arrière-pays peu peuplé à l'époque coloniale française lorsque le territoire faisait partie de l'ancienne Acadie, c'était alors le domaine des premières nations Micmac et Malécite. En 1784, le territoire fut détaché de la Nouvelle-Écosse pour devenir une colonie britannique autonome.

La raison en était qu'il fallait installer d'urgence des milliers d'émigrants en provenance de la Nouvelle- Angleterre qui choisissaient en rester sujets britanniques plutôt que de devenir des citoyens des nouveaux États-Unis d'Amérique. Ce sont les Loyalistes. Or, à peu près au même moment, les descendants des premiers colons, les Acadiens francophones, obtenaient la permission de s'y ré-établir.

À ceux-ci s'ajoutèrent des émigrants venus du Yorkshire ainsi que des familles d'origine allemande qui étaient passées auparavant par la Pennsylvanie. C'est dire le caractère

Former Premier of New Brunswick and Senator Louis J. Robichaud

insolite du peuplement mais c'est ce qui fait du Nouveau-Brunswick un creuset social inusité qui a eu comme résultat de transformer cette future province canadienne en un véritable laboratoire social qui permet d'innover en créant de nouvelles méthodes de cohabitation aussi pacifique que rentable. À tel point que le Nouveau-Brunswick est sans conteste, un exemple pour l'ensemble du Canada.

Le Nouveau-Brunswick, en plus des caractéristiques culturelles diversifiées qui l'ont façonné, jouit une géographie assez spéciale qui le rattache autant à la terre qu'à la mer.

Cette étrange alliance se comprend quand on réalise que 85 pour cent du territoire est constitué de forêts exploitées, et que la province possède un littoral de plus de 2 000 kilomètres.

Par conséquent, on ne saurait s'étonner que la foresterie, la pêche et l'exploitation minière ont été les piliers économiques principaux du Nouveau-Brunswick. Toutefois, à ces industries essentielles, dites primaires, se sont ajoutées depuis quelques année les nouvelles technologies de pointe.

Greenock Church (1824)
St. Andrew's N. B.

Il ne faut pas s'étonner de cet ajout à la panoplie économique; il s'inscrit dans la façon qu'ont mes concitoyens et concitoyennes d'envisager le développement de leur société. Il n'y a pas si longtemps, on démantelait de vieux systèmes périmés de gouvernance pour les remplacer par des structures modernes nettement orientées vers l'avenir, ce qui eut pour résultat d'atténuer les disparités et les rivalités entre la ville et la campagne.

Le Nouveau-Brunswick est, n'en doutez pas, un endroit d'une beauté extraordinaire, en toute saison, mais ce sont ses citoyens et citoyennes qui en ont fait le creuset d'initiatives sociales radicales. Au cours des siècles, nous avons appris, de bon gré, par tâtonnements souvents, à façonner une société distincte qui fait du Nouveau-Brunswick un champ d'action où s'élabore calmement des changements sociétaux importants dans un cadre naturel d'une grande splendeur.

Being neither an historian, nor a poet, when the task might call for those combined talents, I have, nevertheless agreed to introduce the reader to my native province to which I have recently relocated permanently.

That, in itself, should be sufficient an incentive to wax eloquently about the rich history of New Brunswick, her resources, her people and her place in the Canadian federation. After all, someone once wrote that we only speak well of what we love. If this were true- and it is, the temptation to rely on well-worn clichés, however faithful, would be overwhelming. But the story will speak for itself in the pages that follow.

Better, then, to ask a simple question: what distinguishes New Brunswick from her sister provinces and territories? What are the special characteristics that set New Brunswick apart? Paradoxically, the answer is at once easy and difficult: her people and her geography.

New Brunswickers, certainly, share much the same civic virtues and traits that are displayed everywhere. To pretend otherwise would be chauvinistic. However, so many and diverse strains have shaped the development of the Province that the end results have given her a distinctiveness all her own, and in many respects, unique.

A sparsely populated hinterland during the French colonial era when it was part of Acadia, it was the domain of the Micmac and Maliseet First Nations. New Brunswick became a British colonial after-

thought when, in 1784, it was separated from Nova Scotia to stand as an autonomous political entity.

The move was prompted by the urgent need to accommodate thousands of New Englanders who chose to remain British subjects rather than become citizens of the newly independent United States. They were the Loyalists. Coincidentally, at about the same time, the former original settlers, the French Acadians, were allowed to return. Settlers from Yorkshire also came as did Germans by way of Pennsylvania. Thus the stage was set for an unusual and ongoing social experience that has made New Brunswick a veritable social laboratory, a testing ground for new ways to cohabit peacefully, and gainfully, that is a credit to Canada as a whole.

Added to the distinctive cultural traits that have moulded all aspects of her development, New Brunswick also has a peculiar geography that weds her to land and sea. This factor is best understood when one realizes that 85% of her land mass consists of productive forests, while the coastline totals some 2,000 kilometers.

Not surprisingly, forestry, fishing and mining have traditionally formed the basis of industrial development. However, in recent years, the high tech sector is undergoing a phenomenal growth which is quite in keeping with the approach New Brunswickers take to their own development as a community.

Only a few decades ago, they were hard at work shedding old institutions and old ways that had served their

Campebello Island. Roosevelt Park, N. B. This park was jointly established by the Canadian-U.S. governments in 1964 to commemorate US President Franklin D. Roosevelt.

Historic Settlement-King's Landing, N.B. This restored Loyalist village is situated on the lovely sloping banks of the St. John River.

purpose, while creating new ones attuned to the future. In the process, they bridged the gap between urban and rural disparities.

That New Brunswick is a place of sheer beauty, the year round, is undeniable but the fact that her people have made it a crucible for bold social initiatives is what makes her so special in Canada. New Brunswickers have learned over the centuries, by trial and error, to fashion a special society that makes the province an extraordinary work in progress in a natural environment that is second to none.

Historic Settlement – Garden of the Period.

About 33% of New Brunswick's 757,000 people are French speaking. One of the loveliest sights the visitor encounters in Atlantic Canada is the beautiful Acadian flag – which has flown proudly over a warm and talented people. The Acadians faced one of the cruellest events of the colonial period, the tragic deportations of 1755-1763.

New Brunswick has the distinction of being Canada's only officially bilingual province.

Le Pays de la Sagouine at Bouctouche is a fictional village based on the memorable characters invented by internationally renowned Acadian author, Antonine Maillet.

History

The area known as New Brunswick was originally inhabited by tribes of the Algonquian linguistic group. The Mi'kmaq and the Maliseets welcomed the French under Pierre de Monts and Samuel de Champlain when they first landed in New Brunswick in 1604. The early French farmers settled at the head of the Bay of Fundy and up the St. John River Valley as far as present-day Fredericton, and called the land Acadia.

Until the Treaty of Utrecht in 1713, when France ceded the area to Great Britain, both Nova Scotia and New Brunswick were part of Acadia. Fall-out from the English and French wars in Europe forced more than 5,000 Acadians into exile in 1755. Some of them escaped to what was then a remote and uninhabited coastline along the Gulf of St. Lawrence and Chaleur Bay. Today, we call that area the Acadian Peninsula.

Others returned to France or fled to the United States, many settling in Louisiana. The province of New Brunswick, along with Parks Canada has beautifully restored and preserved many of the historic and cultural landmarks of the period.

Fort Beauséjour was originally built by the French in 1751 and taken by the British in 1755 in the battle for control of Acadia. It would later be the scene of another dramatic conflict in the history of Canada, that of the struggle between the young Republic of the United States and the British Empire during the War of 1812.

By 1783 it was the English who were refugees. During the American Revolution, thousands of Loyalist refugees who

Carleton Martello Tower, St. John, N.B.

wanted to remain citizens of the British Empire fled the fledgling republic and settled in the western part of Nova Scotia (now contemporary New Brunswick). So many landed in Saint John that by 1785 they were able to incorporate Canada's first city. In response to loyalist demands for their

Adult gannets have splendid white plumage and grow up to 40 inches (102 cm) in length with a wing span of up to 6 feet (182 cm.)

own Colonial administration, the British government established the new colony of New Brunswick in 1784.

The visitor of today can examine this rich history at the King's Landing Historical Settlement which is located on the beautiful St. John River in the heart of New Brunswick. The spectacular Carleton Martello tower, built in 1814, is yet another example of the drama of these fascinating times.

In 1864, New Brunswick was involved in discussions with the colonies of Nova Scotia, Prince Edward Island and Newfoundland to consider a Maritime union when the Province of Canada issued an invitation to attend the conference in Charlottetown. The result, three years later, was the creation of the Dominion of Canada.

Head Harbour Lighthouse on Campebello Island in the Bay of Fundy.

Wild beavers love carrots. In a pond in Barnesville, east of St. John, Mr. John Mickelburg taught the beavers to obey the command 'come on up'; the beaver would waddle in close to gently grasp the food. His sensitive and intuitive relationship with Canada's best known symbol has rarely, if ever, been replicated.

Anglers flock to the renowned salmon rivers of New Brunswick, such as the Miramichi, Restigouche, Nepisiquit, Salmon, St. Croix and Tobique.

Agriculture is as important to New Brunswick's economy as its traditional family values are to its social fabric. The province is famous for its potatoes; its seed potatoes are exported to over 30 million countries in the world.
(see photo p. 129).

Fishing for salmon on the Miramichi river.

Fredericton Legislative Building. This dignified, stately seat of government with its classical dome is a reflection of the quiet elegance of the capital of New Brunswick. The historic buildings and tree-lined expanses nearly make one forget that the scope of the province's knowledge and information technology sectors is so advanced.

A Jewellery case of Natural Beauty
Where the Spirit of History and the Heartbeat of the Future live as One.

L'honorable Lise Thibault a choisi d'illustrer son texte de présentation par des œuvres d'artistes-peintres contemporains qui parcourent le Québec et s'inspirent de la grande diversité de ses attraits pour exprimer leur art.

La Cathédrale de Montréal.

L'Anse St-Jean.

Après midi d'hiver.

QUÉBEC

Us et coutumes.

The Honorable Lise Thibault
Lieutenant-gouverneur du
Québec

Tant de visages sous un même nom, tant de facettes à un même diamant. On aurait envie de dire «Les Québec» plutôt que «Le Québec». Riche en contrastes, chacune des régions qui le composent rivalise de beauté. Tels les pigments que les impressionnistes s'ingéniaient à appliquer sur leur toile, le résultat de l'exercice donne naissance à un tableau magnifique. Oui, la province de Québec est magnifique. Elle porte en elle les rivières comme les lacs, le fleuve comme la mer, les plaines comme les montagnes. Elle est nature sauvage, rurale autant qu'urbaine. Elle se couvre de neige blanche ou se pare de vert tendre et de pourpre. La parcourir, c'est se laisser entraîner à travers une mosaïque d'images extraordinaires.

Le français, coloré par des accents acadiens, irlandais, écossais ou anglais, est parlé par plus de 80% de la population québécoise. Ainsi, chaque région porte les reflets de son histoire. Berceau de la Nouvelle-France, le Québec a préservé cette langue poétique malgré l'émergence anglaise, au milieu du XVIIIe siècle. Par ailleurs, des noms de villes, de cours d'eau et de lieux affichent encore leur appellation d'origine amérindienne, comme en fait foi le mot «Québec» (passage étroit). De ces Premières Nations, nous avons également appris que la sève des érables avait la particularité de devenir un extraordinaire sirop d'une saveur incomparable, à présent recherché partout dans le monde. Mais surtout, la production du sirop d'érable symbolise l'arrivée du printemps. Par milliers, nous nous rendons gaiement déguster les mets traditionnels dans l'ambiance chaleureuse de nos cabanes à sucre, au milieu des érablières.

Certaines grandes villes du Québec arborent un indé-

Les Îles de Mai.

niable cachet européen. Tels d'immenses plateaux de cinéma, on croirait que des rues entières ont été importées de France ou d'Angleterre pour décorer le site enchanteur près duquel on les a ancrées. Car parler du Québec sans nommer le fleuve Saint-Laurent, c'est laisser dans son écrin un joyau dont tous les Québécois parlent avec fierté. Nombre de villes et de villages le bordent, offrant un point d'horizon vers lequel il fait bon rêver. De part en part, le Saint-Laurent traverse le sud du Québec pour s'élargir en un golfe se jetant dans l'océan Atlantique. Ses eaux reflètent autant les gratte-ciel de Montréal que le Rocher Percé de la Gaspésie. Entre ces deux points, mille kilomètres de ruban bleu se déroulent avec grâce.

Si j'avais un seul mot pour vous décrire les Québécois, j'utiliserais sans hésiter celui de l'hospitalité. Latins de souche, ils aiment recevoir et animer leurs fêtes historiques et festivals autour d'un bon repas. De leurs ancêtres, ils aiment évoquer la mémoire, honorant ainsi le «Je me souviens» de notre devise emblématique. Nous comprenons donc facilement que le secteur touristique occupe une large part dans l'activité économique provinciale.

Le Québec a la chance de savoir sa terre riche et fertile. Riche par sa composition, dont les gisements miniers ont donné naissance à plusieurs villes, ainsi que par ses champs propres à la culture. Riche par ses forêts composées d'essences d'arbres de grande qualité dont on tire papier et bois en abondance. Leur superficie exploitable couvrirait toute la France ! Riche par ses terres, capables de cultiver des produits alimentaires de grande qua-

lité. Riche aussi par ses eaux produisant une énergie électrique envoyée de son grand voisin du sud, les États-Unis. La réserve d'eau potable du Québec porte le troisième rang au niveau mondial !

Malgré l'exploitation de ces ressources naturelles, le XXe siècle, sous les effets d'un fort courant d'industrialisation et de modernité, n'a pu empêcher un exode massif au profit des zones urbaines du Québec. Ainsi, la grande région de Montréal, métropole québécoise, se partagea la vedette avec celle de Québec, la capitale, pour accueillir un grand nombre de citoyens avides d'études et de travail. Les années trente virent aussi de nombreuses familles du sud de la province partir à des centaines de kilomètres plus au nord, afin de défricher une nouvelle région remplie de promesses, l'Abitibi-Témiscamingue. De nos jours, l'ensemble des régions du Québec accueille annuellement des milliers d'immigrants venus tenter de réaliser leur «rêve américain». Car le Québec, c'est aussi l'Amérique, jouissant d'un mariage de cultures incomparable.

Économiquement parlant, le Québec a développé des secteurs de pointe uniques. Cela créa une importante demande d'exportation de ses produits et services. Les domaines de l'aéronautique et de la bio-tech-

nologie s'illustrent brillamment sur la scène des marchés mondiaux. Les Québécois sont de fameux innovateurs et créateurs! Je leur dis souvent, lors de rencontres, qu'oser la vie, c'est trouver des «autrement» remplis d'espoir. Leur esprit d'entrepreneurship et leur flexibilité favorisent certainement cette ouverture d'esprit nécessaire pour développer et rechercher de nouvelles façons de faire, d'agir et de réfléchir. La région de la Beauce est réputée pour son sens de l'innovation et son esprit d'entreprise.

J'ai beaucoup de respect et d'admiration envers les créateurs d'ici. Ils peuvent tout autant capter la luminosité du soleil sur les espaces enneigés, que la faible lueur du réverbère sur l'asphalte mouillé d'une ruelle de ville. Plusieurs d'entre eux sont des inconditionnels de la superbe région de Charlevoix, sans cesse à l'affût de nouvelles compositions où montagnes, fleuve et maisons canadiennes se marient à l'infini. D'autres évoluent

L'hiver en fête.

La route de René Richard.

sous un amalgame de couleurs et de formes plus éclatées, pour arriver à livrer leur vision moderne de l'art pictural et sculptural.

Dans les autres domaines artistiques, les Dieux des Arts se firent également généreux. On ne pourrait passer sous silence l'immense talent musical et vocal de notre province. Combien de chanteurs de réputation internationale et même mondiale, viennent du Québec? Des chefs d'orchestre, des musiciens et des voix lyriques exceptionnelles ont circulé autour du monde. Des auteurs dramatiques et littéraires voient leurs œuvres traduites et diffusées dans des dizaines de langues. Dans la francophonie, les noms de Gilles Vigneault et Félix Leclerc portent l'étendard de notre poésie. Que de sources vivifiantes !

J'aime servir au sein du Québec. Quel privilège que de côtoyer des citoyens si généreux et si vivants ! Le Québec est le berceau de la démocratie en Amérique et c'est encore sous

cette forme gouvernementale qu'elle se gère aujourd'hui. Depuis 1975, notre province s'est aussi enrichie de la Charte québécoise des droits et libertés où il est reconnu officiellement que la personne est titulaire de certaines libertés et de certains droits fondamentaux. Cela procure une vie de société où le pouvoir s'exerce de façon démocratique et où le droit prime la force. Les droits fondamentaux consacrés par la Charte touchent le droit à la vie, à l'intégrité et à la liberté, le droit à la sauvegarde de la personne et de la réputation, le droit au respect et à la vie privée, le droit à la jouissance paisible de ses biens, le droit à l'inviolabilité de la demeure et le droit au secret professionnel. Tous ces droits ont été établis en vue d'assurer une qualité de vie aux Québécois. Oui, avec le Québec, le Canada possède un véritable joyau où il fait bon vivre et œuvrer en toute dignité, en toute liberté.

English Translation

So many faces to a single name, so many facets to a diamond. It would be tempting to say 'the Québecs' rather than 'Québec', a land so rich in contrasts, with each region as beautiful as the next. As the pigments that impressionist painters so deftly applied to their canvas, the result gave birth to a magnificent scenery. Yes, the province of Québec is magnificent. It carries in its bosom, rivers as well as lakes, plains as well as mountains, and an ocean. Side by side, wilderness, countryside and cities coexist. With the passing seasons, the province is covered with bright white snow, soft green or crimson leaves. To travel across Québec is synonymous with letting yourself be taken through a patchwork of extraordinary images.

French, tinged with Acadian, Irish, Scottish or English accents, is the language spoken by 80% of the Québec population, each region thus carrying the memory of its past history. As the cradle of New France, Québec has managed to preserve its poetic language despite the emergence of English in the mid-1700s. Otherwise, names of cities, rivers and localities still bear their original Amerindian names, with the word Québec* (narrow passage) as proof. From these First Nations, we also learned that the sap from maple trees could be transformed into a most flavorful syrup, now internationally renowned. But above all, the production of maple syrup symbolizes the onset of Spring when Quebecers gingerly flock by the thousands to savour traditional dishes in the warm setting of sugarhouses erected amidst groves of maple trees.

Some large cities in Québec have an undeniable European flavour. One would think that, much like a huge movie set, entire streets have been dropped here from France or England to better decorate the enchanting surroundings of the St. Lawrence. Indeed, talking about Québec without mentioning the St. Lawrence River is like leaving in its jewelry case a gem of which Quebecers are so proud. Numerous cities and villages are erected along its banks, offering a veritable dreamscape. From end to end, the St. Lawrence flows through the South of Québec, widening into a gulf that empties into the Atlantic Ocean. Its waters reflect Montréal skyscrapers and Gaspesia's Rocher Percé alike. Between these two geographical points, a thousand-kilometer blue ribbon flows gracefully.

If I could only use one word to describe Quebecers, it would be hospitality. Of Latin ancestry, Quebecers love to have people over for a meal and to organize historical events and festivals where food is plentiful. They like to recall the memory of their ancestors, thus honoring the province's motto "Je me souviens" which means "I remember". No wonder the tourist industry plays such a large part in the province's economic activities.

Québec is blessed with rich and fertile soil. Rich in its makeup including mineral deposits which led to the development of numerous cities, as well as fields for farming. Rich in forests abounding in high grade trees yielding vast quantities of paper and wood. It is said that the harvestable extent of our forests would cover all of France! Rich in soil able to yield top quality food products. Also rich in waters which produce electrical energy that is the envy of the United States, our large neighbour to the South. Moreover, Québec's drinking water reserves rank third in the world.

Despite the exploitation of these natural resources, the twentieth century, swept by a strong current of industrialization and modernization, could not stop a massive exodus of people to the urban centres of the province. The Greater Montréal region, Québec's largest city, shares equal billing with Québec City, our Capital city, in welcoming a great number of citizens wishing to pursue their studies or to find work. Also, during the nineteen thirties, families from the southern part of the province left their native homes to migrate hundreds of kilometers North to the Abitibi-Témiscamingue region in order to clear this new land full of promise. Today, all of Québec's regions welcome thousands of immigrants every year, who would like to turn their 'American Dream' into reality. Because Québec is indeed part of America and, as such, it presents a wonderful tapestry of cultures and diversity.

The Basilica of Notre-Dame in Old Montréal is one of North America's most splendid churches as well as one of its largest – it holds 5000 people. The church was built between 1824 and 1829 and its neo-gothic style is reminiscent of some of the great European cathedrals.

Laurentians – Autumn with Village.

Economically speaking, Québec has developed unique leading-edge sectors. This has led to a great demand in the export of its products and services. The aeronautics and biotechnology sectors rank among the best on the international scene – Quebecers are amazingly creative and innovative. At meetings, I often tell people that daring to live means finding "better and different ways" of doing things. Their entrepreneurial spirit and flexibility certainly contribute to the open mindedness necessary to find and develop new ways of doing, acting and thinking. The Beauce region is particularly known for its entrepreneurship and sense of innovation.

I have immense respect and admiration for Québec's creative minds. They can catch the sun's rays on vast snowy grounds just as deftly as the faint reflection of a street lamp on the slippery wet asphalt of an alley in the city. Many of them are unconditional lovers of the majestic Charlevoix region, constantly searching for new compositions where mountains, rivers and Canadian homes intermix perfectly, in an endless variety of ways. Others show their talent using bolder colors and forms to render their own modern vision of pictorial or sculptural art.

Quebecers are also gifted in many other artistic fields. I would be remiss were I not to mention the province's great musical and vocal talent. Numerous vocal artists of international reputation come from Québec. Conductors, musicians and exceptional lyric voices have circled the globe. Playwrights' and writers' works are translated and published in dozens of languages. In the francophone communities, the names of Gilles Vigneault and Félix Leclerc are synonymous with Québec poetry. What inspiring models!

I have the distinct privilege of serving my fellow Quebecers, for it is indeed a privilege to live among such generous and lively citizens. Québec was and is the cradle of democracy in America. Since 1975, it has also been enriched with the Charter of Human Rights and Freedoms which officially recognizes that an individual possesses intrinsic liberties and fundamental rights. Our society is one where power is exercised democratically and where rights prevail over force. The fundamental rights enshrined in the Charter state that a person has a right to life, integrity and freedom, a right to the safeguard of his dignity, honour and reputation, a right to respect for his private life, a right to peaceful enjoyment of his property, a right to the inviolability of his home, and a right to non-disclosure of confidential information. All of these rights were established in order to ensure quality of life for all Quebecers. Yes, in Canada, Québec is a veritable gem where the living is good and where it is possible to work in total dignity and freedom.

The Saint Lawrence River is one of the most important rivers in North America. From its source in the Great Lakes, it flows through a vast estuary and the Gulf of Saint Lawrence to the Atlantic. Roughly 1,200 km in length, it is one of the leading navigable waterways of the world and the main river route in North America.

History

In 1534, the King of France sent Jacques Cartier to explore the vast land and oceans of Terre-Neuve, believing it was time for France to find and conquer a golden Empire as the Spanish had in Mexico and Peru. Cartier explored and mapped in meticulous detail, assigning place names everywhere he went. When he began to explore the mighty St. Lawrence River, he asked the aboriginal people what they called their land. 'Canada', they told him, a word that meant village in their language. Believing this to be the name of the whole country, he put 'Canada' on the map.

Sailing on into the Gulf of the St Lawrence, his arrival was heralded to the nearby village of Stadacona (now Québec City). Cartier was amazed at the sight of the great cliffs rising high over a river which was the gateway to a continent. Perhaps even more astonishing was his meeting with Chief Donnacona whose people were fascinated by the strangers with the pointed magic sticks and travelled in great wooden houses that moved over the water.

When the strangers erected a cross on the shore, Donnacona understood that they were claiming his people's ancestral lands. Though the great chief protested in an angry speech from his canoe, it was clear that Cartier and his band did not understand.

At the end of Cartier's second trip to what would become New France, Cartier seized the chief and took him back to France, where he would die, never again seeing his homeland.

Cartier would complete his missions to Canada bitterly disappointed. Many decades would pass before the great cartographer and explorer Samuel de Champlain would sail up the St. Lawrence, gazing upon the serene meadows where Stadacona once stood.

"You could hardly hope to find a more beautiful country", he said. Five years later, in 1608, he would bring settlers to stay at the Habitation of Quebec. The founder of New France (which would become the province of Québec) would

Scientist checking a new born seal pup on Magdalen Islands.

become one of the most famous explorers of all time.

Nearly 150 years later, during the wars between the colonial powers, the English armies under General James Wolfe laid siege to Québec and would defeat the French troops under General Louis-Joseph Montcalm on September 13, 1759, in the battle of the Plains of Abraham.

This was by no means an easy victory as they faced a formidable opponent in the brave Montcalm, who had already won a bloody victory against the British at Ticonderoga a year earlier. In that same summer of 1758, however, the British beseiged and captured the fortress of Louisbourg.

In 1759, one British army marched on Montreal from the west, while another marched from the south. At the same time, General James Wolfe's seaborn invasion brought his army to the gates of Quebec. The daring General Wolfe smouldered in frustration, as he was unable to attack the city standing on the invulnerable cliffs of Quebec.

At summer's end, Wolfe decided to

A view of the Landing Place above the Town of Québec, ca 1759.

attack upriver, beyond the city. On the night of September 12, he landed his soldiers at the foot of the cliffs and they scrambled to the top without being seen. By dawn, Wolfe's army stood on the Plains of Abraham. General Montcalm came out to face them, with a vastly depleted and exhausted army. Bravely, the French attacked the British and were cut down where they stood. General Wolfe would die on the battlefield after learning of the historic victory. General Montcalm died early the next morning. In 1760, Montréal fell to the British troops.

In 1763, under the Treaty of Paris, the King of France ceded Canada and all its territories to the King of England. In 1774 The Québec Act recognized the use of French civil law and the seigniorial system in the broad expanses of Britain's most recent colony, which, at the time, included the Great Lakes and Ohio.

Rebellions against undemocratic goverment in 1837, in both Upper and Lower Canada, led to the Act of Union of 1840. At the time, Québec became part of the Province of Canada, and would be known as Canada East, along with neighbouring Ontario (Canada West). Québec would become a separate province of the Dominion of Canada at the time of Confederation in 1867.

Québec City – Nowhere else in North America is the appearance and atmosphere of an old-world city so complete. The entire old section of the town was declared an UNESCO World Heritage Site in 1985.

Percé Rock, Gaspe. This massive offshore rock, marked by reddish-gold limestone is the highpoint of the scenic splendor of the south coast of the Gaspé peninsula.

The joie de vivre of Montréal defies all superlatives. This photo shows the mixture of old and new in this vibrant, exciting city, rich in history, culture, and old world charm. With a population of three million, Montréal has become one of the world's major cities.

Québec has an area of 1,700,000 km and is three times as big as France, five times as big as Japan, and seven times the size of Great Britain. Another way of looking at it? Québec is one-sixth the size of Canada's total land mass.

Parc de la Jacques Cartier – this monumentally beautiful park is 40 kilometres (25 miles) north of Québec City. Malak has captured the enormous silence and colour of this wilderness area. High rising hills and winding rivers with whitewater stretches are found in an area of just a few miles.

An Economic Powerhouse Where the Miracle of Nature is Only a Whisper Away.

The CN Tower, at 553.33 meters or 1,815 ft. 5 inches is the world's tallest freestanding structure. It attracts over two million visitors each year.

ONTARIO

The greatest value of heritage lies in what it brings to our individual lives. Whether the experience involves walking in the wilderness, unearthing ancient artifacts, or restoring fine examples of architecture, an appreciation of heritage is intrinsic to our quality of life. In our increasingly global world, heritage is a necessary counterbalance because it seeks to preserve much of what is important to us and the communities in which we live.

Heritage conservation involves selecting those parts of our heritage that we wish to save and taking practical steps to conserve them. It is now recognized as a three-stage process that proceeds from identification, through protection and preservation, to interpretation and use. A comprehensive approach integrates many disciplines including, for example, the knowledge and expertise of archaeologists, architects, biologists, historians, museologists, urban planners and property managers.

Ontario is Canada's second largest province in size, covering over one

million square kilometres, nearly 160,000 square kilometres of which are taken up by Ontario's 250,000 freshwater lakes. 11.8 million of the nation's 30.95 million people are centered here, largely clustered in cities, towns and villages along the southern part of the province.

Ontario is a province of diverse cultures, with an exciting history. Its heritage is celebrated by communities large and small. At annual harvest festivals in small communities, War of 1812 battle re-enactments, First Nation gatherings, Underground Railroad tours, Highland games, Oktoberfest celebrations, solemn commemorations of natural or man-made disasters, and visits to historic homes and districts, people rejoice in their common and disparate heritages.

The Ontario Heritage Foundation was created by the provincial government in 1967 as part of its centennial celebration of Canada's Confederation. Today, the Foundation, as the lead provincial heritage agency, works with communities across Ontario to accomplish its mission of identifying, preserving, protecting and promoting Ontario's rich, natural and cultural heritage. Partnerships are central to our work — partnerships with the corporate world, other heritage organizations and individuals. Our partners and volunteers provide interpretation at many of our sites, raise funds, hold special events, and in some cases act as custodians.

The Foundation is also unique among the many heritage organizations in the province, in that its man-

Mr. Allan Gottlieb is past Chairman of the Canada Council and former Canadian Ambassador to the United States. A Companion of the Order of Canada, he is currently Chairman of the Ontario Heritage Foundation.

date encompasses natural, built and cultural heritage.

The Foundation holds in trust for the people of Ontario and Canada 22 built heritage sites, 11 of which are also historic sites of national importance. Over 100 natural heritage properties, including 60 along the Bruce Trail on the Niagara Escarpment, a UNESCO World Biosphere Reserve of international importance, are open to the public for recreational or passive use. 199 conservation easement agreements protect significant architectural or natural heritage features of properties in perpetuity. And over 1,100 historical plaques across Ontario tell the stories of the people, places and events that have shaped our history.

Our work extends to every corner of the province. We are a trustee and pro-

The Flat Iron building in Toronto is a beautifully restored Victorian red brick architectural landmark which stands as part of another age amidst shining skyscrapers.

The Elgin Theatre, as it appears today, restored to its original grandeur. With its richly gilded and marbleized surfaces, this theatre was the first in Toronto to offer such opulent décor. (compliments of the Ontario Heritage Foundation.)

tector of built and natural heritage, a custodian of cultural and archaeological collections, the operator of heritage-related businesses and a leader in heritage education and outreach.

Our properties range from a restored 19th-century pharmacy, the Niagara Apothecary in Niagara-on-the-Lake, to Fulford Place, a superb example of Edwardian opulence, to The Hudson's Bay Company Staff and Servant Houses in Moose Factory, a far corner of northern Ontario. The Elgin and Winter Garden Theatre Centre in Toronto, built in 1913 and restored by the Foundation in the 1980s, is the last operating double-decker theatre in the world.

Public education is central to our mission. Exhibitions, conferences, seminars, publications and innovative uses of technology foster learning and information sharing that encourage active participation in keeping our legacy alive and vital.

Heritage education and cultural preservation are supported through several province-wide programs. The provincial plaque program commemorates the great people, places, and events that have historical and cultural significance. The Heritage Community Recognition Program acknowledges individuals who have made significant contributions to heritage preservation in their communities. The Young Heritage Leaders program honours young people for their contributions to preserving local history and encourages them to continue their interest in Ontario's heritage.

As diverse as the heritage of this great province, is the range of volunteers and partners who work together to interpret that legacy for visitors and residents alike. We urge you to share the 'heritage impulse' — sample the natural, built and cultural heritage that Ontario has to offer, and discover why we are so proud of our province.

The Niagara Apothecary was acquired by the Ontario Heritage Foundation and has been beautifully restored to the delight of the millions who visit the Niagara region.

One in three Canadians live in Ontario, Canada's second largest and most populous province, which is the size of France and Spain combined. The largest concentration of people and cities is clustered in what is called 'The Golden Horseshoe' along the western shore of Lake Ontario, including the Greater Toronto region.

History

The modern, multicultural face of Ontario is just the most recent chapter in a centuries old process of immigration which started in the early 17th century with the voyage of Henry Hudson, who claimed the Hudson Bay area for Britain in 1611.

But the area which was to become Ontario was first inhabited by the Algonquian and Iroquoian speaking tribes, which were highly developed politically and culturally by the time the Europeans penetrated the area.

(Ontario means sparkling or beautiful water, in the language of the Iroquois and, as there are about 250,000 lakes in the province, this in no way overstates the case.)

Samuel de Champlain and Étienne Brûlé first established contact with the Indians of southern Ontario in 1613. The Huron Confederacy of the period was made up of prosperous farmers whose homeland of more than 20,000 people was located on a small peninsula on Georgian Bay, in Lake Huron.

European settlement would gradu-

ally develop over time, with one of the most significant events being the arrival of the United Empire Loyalists in 1784. The Loyalists, who began to farm in the St. Lawrence, Lake Ontario, and Niagara regions fled the 13 colonies (later the United States of America) after the American Revolutionary wars. They disliked the very idea of a Republic and wanted to remain loyal to the monarchy.

But soon, Britain and the United States went to war again in July, 1812. The Americans decided to punish

Britain by invading and conquering British North America, particularly Upper Canada.

General Isaac Brock, who commanded the British troops in Upper Canada, had no intention of allowing the Americans to take the colony.

When the war began, he went on the attack, forging an alliance with Tecumseh of the Shawnee, whose warriors fought side by side with British and colonial troops. Tecumseh was a veteran of many battles to protect the homelands of the aboriginal peoples of the Great Lakes against American settlers.

In August, 1812, Tecumseh and Brock forced an American surrender at Detroit. This was the battle that may have changed the course of the

Battle of Queenston Heights, 13 October, 1812.

war as it inspired the Canadians, who began to believe that victory was possible.

By the fall of 1812, the Americans crossed the Niagara River and seized the heights above the village of Queenston. This time, Upper Canadian volunteers and their native allies fought shoulder to shoulder with the British regulars. Queenston Heights was retaken, but the courageous General Brock was not there to share in the victory.

He had been shot dead in a desperate charge up the Heights. Brock's legacy remains a powerful one in the annals of the fascinating history of Canada and the province of Ontario. In fact, his statue stands on guard for Canada, the hero's gaze fixed in perpetual vigilance on the great Republic to the south.

Tecumseh was killed in 1813 at the Battle of Moraviantown, Upper Canada. The British preserved what was to become Ontario from American visions of manifest destiny, but the Shawnees and other aboriginal nations

lost their own war and much of their land.

Several decades later, the Loyalists, accustomed to autonomy in the American colonies, demanded changes in their new homeland. Rebellions against undemocratic government in 1837, in both Upper and Lower Canada, prompted the British to send Lord Durham to report on the troubles.

As a result of Durham's recommendations, the Act of Union of 1840 joined Upper and Lower Canada once again, this time as the Province of Canada. Although a more democratic and responsible government resulted, the union was not a success: Canada East and Canada West continued to be two distinct regions. They entered the confederation conference of 1864 as though they were separate, and became different provinces – Ontario and Quebec – at Confederation in 1867.

Sir John A. Macdonald of Ontario became Canada's first Prime Minister.

Brock's Monument at Queenston, Ont.

Fulford Place, Brockville is a superb example of Edwardian opulence and a tribute to the work of the Ontario Heritage Foundation.

The beautiful city of Kingston, which lies on the north shore of Lake Ontario, is one of the oldest, culturally rich cities in Canada.

London is a pleasant university town and major industrial centre all in one. St. Peter's Cathedral is a reflection of the dignity and quiet grandeur of this city of tree lined streets.

Flower Pot Island in Lake Huron's magnificent Georgian Bay was once covered by water and the caves high up on the cliffs attest to the height of ancient water levels. It is named for this pillar of eroded limestone, 17 metres(55 ft.) high.

Point Pelee National Park lies at the most southernmost point on the Canadian mainland and is famous as an area where two major bird migration routes converge

Lady slipper.

146

Canada geese – In the fall and spring, people all across Canada thrill to the high-flying 'V' formation and distant honking of our national bird.

The Mennonites were early settlers to the Kitchener-Waterloo area and these highly successful farmers can still be seen going to Meeting in horse drawn buggies.

This area of great scenic beauty is found in an 80 kilometer stretch of the St. Lawrence river and is divided by the Canada-U.S. border. Its sparkling waters, dotted with thousands of little islands of pink granite, are a paradise for sailors.

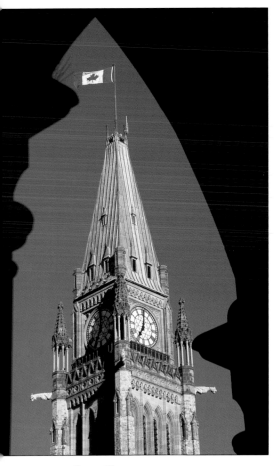

Peace Tower.

Changing of the Guard.

Skyline of Ottawa.

Welcome to Ottawa, Canada's national capital.

As Mayor of the fourth largest city in Canada, and on behalf of all the residents of Ottawa, I am honoured to introduce our nation's Capital to Canadians from coast to coast – as well as to the thousands of visitors who tour our beautiful country.

This is a city which treasures and preserves its proud history. The ornate halls of our Parliament buildings and the institutions which make up the seat of the federal government of Canada find their home on the towering cliffs overlooking the Ottawa river. Visitors from around the world come to admire the vice-regal official residence of the Governor General of Canada, and thrill to the awe-inspiring pagentry of the Changing of the Guard. Our museums, galleries, and theatres are unsurpassed. I think of the National Arts Centre and the Canadian Museum of Civilization, the Museum of Nature, the Museum of Science and Technology and so many other wonderful venues that showcase the nation's history, its culture and heritage.

But just as Ottawa honours its past, so it embraces its future. Indeed over the past fifty years, confident and cosmopolitan Ottawa has successfully transformed itself into the advanced-technology capital of Canada. The Ottawa region, strategically located at the centre of Canada's commercial heartland, boasts a bilingual, highly skilled and educated workforce – imaginative, talented and entrepreneurial people who have diversified, modernized and expanded the region's economy.

Ottawa was once a lumber town,

then a government town. Today it is a dynamic, prosperous, business-oriented community and a world leader in high technology. In the Ottawa region, the public and private sectors work together as partners to create a powerful centre for investment, innovation, and entrepreneurship.

At the same time, Ottawa is considered to be one of the loveliest and most liveable cities in Canada. It is a clean, green and safe city; home to active and healthy lifestyles. Our wealth of parks, forests, waterways and open spaces – with hundreds of kilometres of cross-country ski trails and biking paths – all translate into a superb quality of life for all of our citizens. Just minutes from the downtown area are some of the region's finest golf courses and ski hills, along with the pristine lakes that dot cottage country. And surrounding the urban core is the 205 square mile 'emerald necklace', a unique and precious gem of federally owned open spaces. No wonder Ottawa is praised as one of the greenest capitals of the world.

In winter, our famed canal is a magical ice covered skating rink; the longest in the world.Cutting through the heart of the city, this shimmering surface is a meeting place for thousands of outdoor lovers and their families.

In summer, our hot air balloons fill the skies over the city with a kaleidoscope of colour. And in the Springtime, the famed Canadian tulip festival opens to coincide with the eagerly awaited spendor of over two million bulbs – a joyous riot of shades of yellows and gold, pinks and reds and purples.

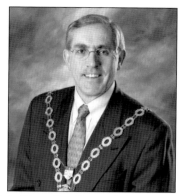

Bob Chiarelli, Mayor of Ottawa

The Ottawa Board of Trade, with the assistance of renowned photographer Malak, whose photographs immortalized the tulip, has held the Festival since 1953.

Malak, whose work is held in permanent exhibit at Ottawa's Rideau Club and the Ottawa Airport, as well as being displayed at the Museum of Civilization and the Museum of Nature, among others, was an Officer of the Order of Canada and held an honourary key to our beautiful city. His award winning photography has been the subject of eight books and innumerable articles, delighting the eye and touching the heart of generations of Canadians.

In many ways Malak, a man of grace and dignity, personified the city in which he lived, with his talented partner and wife, Barbara, for so many years. Both Malak and Barbara have taken profound pride in the nation's Capital, in its history and its magnificent potential. It is a great privilege to introduce the City of Ottawa in this lovely volume – of which he is the distinguished photo editor – and which has been dedicated to the memory of one of our finest citizens.

Rideau Falls.

Museum of Contemporary Photography and Chateau Laurier along Rideau Canal and Locks.

Ice Sculpture of Bird.

Skating on the Rideau Canal.

National Arts Centre.

Parliament Buildings in Winter.

Tulips and Little Girl.

151

"The Giant Plain
Open, Immense, yet Tender
and Full of Dreams." (Gabrielle Roy)

The unique growing conditions in southern Manitoba have made the province the sunflower belt. Manitoba produces over 70% of Canada's sunflower seed.

The area now known as Riding Mountain Park was inhabited for well over 6,000 years by Canada's aboriginal people and is now home to an astonishing variety of wildlife and bird species, and the buffalo roam freely.

MANITOBA

Nestled in the Canadian heartland – between Ontario and Saskatchewan – Manitoba is a province of great pride and diversity. It is just over 250,000 square miles in size, with a population approaching 1.2 million.

As you travel through the cities and towns that make up "Friendly Manitoba," from the United States border all the way to the territory of Nunavut, the landscape changes from rolling hills to fields of waving grain; from rushing rivers to a huge inland sea and 100,000 lakes; from bright city lights to northern tundra and unspoiled wilderness.

This diversity allows for a great variety of things to see and do. Winnipeg is Manitoba's capital city and it boasts a vibrant arts and entertainment scene, fine restaurants, state-of-the-art shopping centres,

charming historical sites and districts, and world-class gaming facilities. Discover the peace and tranquility of rural Manitoba's white sandy beaches, great boating and fishing, and an exciting array of winter activities including cross-country skiing and snowmobiling. And explore the vast northern region of the province with its awesome scenic beauty and incredible natural resources. The northern port of Churchill on Hudson Bay draws tourists from around the world to see the polar bear and beluga whale.

The population of Manitoba is as diverse as its physical environment. This is a province with a rich blend of people of all origins and ancestries, where we celebrate each other's cultures. Always count on the warmth and hospitality of Manitobans,

The Honorable Peter M. Liba, C.M. O.M. is the Lieutenant Governor of Manitoba

whether you are attending one of the many fairs and festivals that run year-round, or stopping for a night or two at a bed-and-breakfast in a small prairie town.

This is Manitoba – the heart of the continent, in the centre of Canada – a province we truly treasure.

Manitobans are proud of their superb beaches in a province of over 100,000 lakes. Lake Winnipeg is Canada's fifth largest lake, and the spectacular Grand Beach is a natural treasure.

Pisew Falls on the Grass River, Manitoba.

History

The Assiniboine Indians were the first inhabitants of Manitoba. Other tribes included the nomadic Cree who were buffalo hunters. In their search for the spice-rich Orient through the Northwest Passage, Europeans reached Manitoba through Hudson Bay in the early 17th century. Unlike most of the rest of Canada, the northern parts of the province were settled before the south.

Charles II of England granted the Hudson's Bay Company a large tract of land named Rupert's Land. The company set up fur-trading posts to exploit the country's wealth. Among their major posts were York Factory at the mouths of the Nelson and Hayes Rivers, and Prince of Wales's Fort at the mouth of the mighty Churchill.

Later, traders from New France would push across the southern part of Manitoba. They were succeeded by teams of English-speaking "pedlars" and French-Canadian voyageurs who paddled swift canoes from Montreal to the West and back, seeking furs.

Intense rivalry for furs developed between the Montreal-based North West Company and the Hudson's Bay Company. Alexander Mackenzie, an employee of the North West Company, pushed the chain of forts west into the Rocky Mountains and north to the Arctic. The rivalry came to its height in the Red River and Assiniboine River Valleys in Manitoba, where open warfare broke out.

Fort Garry, at the forks of the two rivers, was the centre of the Hudson's Bay Company's fur trade at Red River. Later, the company built Lower Fort Garry, 30 kilometres away. Lower Fort Garry still stands, but it was the fort at the forks of the rivers that grew into the city of Winnipeg.

In the 1860s, the Province of Canada, anxious to expand into the great northwest, asked Britain to buy out the Hudson's Bay Company. Although willing to request the surrender of the land from the Hudson's Bay Company, Britain insisted that the money come from Canada. Canada

The highlight in the Manitoba Museum of Man and Nature is the replica of the Nonsuch, a ship that sailed in search of furs from England to Hudson's Bay in 1668.

offered the company 300,000 pounds sterling. The company settled for the money, plus one twentieth of all the fertile land in the west and the land that surrounded their trading posts.

The inhabitants of the area were not consulted on this transaction. No clear terms were spelled out for the people of the Red River area and, during negotiations on their status, resistance developed in the colony. The Métis, a mostly French-speaking people of mixed European and Indian blood, rallied under the leadership of Louis Riel to oppose the Canadian proposals. Riel succeeded in uniting both the French and English-speaking groups to establish a locally elected, provisional government in 1869.

Negotiations between the provisional government and the government of Canada led to Parliament passing the Manitoba Act of 1870, under which Manitoba joined the other provinces in Confederation.

The new province consisted of 36,000 square kilometres surrounding the Red River Valley. It was called the "postage stamp" province because of its square shape and relatively small size.

However, the province did not remain that small. Its boundaries were enlarged in 1881 and again in 1912. Today, Manitoba is 650,000 square kilometres and could have been larger had it not been for an 1884 decision in favour of Ontario, which established the present-day boundary between the two provinces.

Lower Fort Garry.

Manitoba is the eastern-most of the three prairie provinces and gateway to western Canada. As the visitor begins to drive across the great plains of the prairies, the tall, colourfully painted grain elevators, and the infinite blue skies which characterize the western plains come into view.

Agriculture is big business in Manitoba, providing employment for 1 in 9 Manitobans and contributing billions of dollars to the provincial economy.

Golden wheat fields under infinite blue skies.

Grant's Old Grist Mill, Sturgeon Creek, Winnipeg. A replica of an original watermill built in 1829 which may have been the first instance of the use of hydro power in Manitoba.

Travellers along the western shore of Lake Winnipeg will find forests of spruce and scotch pine and lakes of pristine tranquillity.

Greek Orthodox church, Winnipeg, Manitoba.

*Kildonan Park,
Winnipeg.*

Manitoba is a multicultural mix of people from every continent and virtually every country in the world. The well known author, Hugh MacLennan, wrote that: "Today the Red River Valley is no longer the 'West'; it is the geographical heart of Canada. It may also be the ethnic and social heart as well."

*Souris Swing Bridge,
Souris, Man.*

Winnipeg is often described as the place where the west begins; it is a city of great ethnic diversity with a lively, cultural life. It is also a city of trees; estimates range up to two million!

The Forks, at the historic juncture of the Red and Assiniboine rivers, was named as such by European fur traders centuries ago and remains a favourite gathering place.

The Golden Boy which crowns the Legislative Building is 4 meters high and weighs 5 tons. This icon of Manitoba is coated in 23.5 karat gold and carries, fittingly, a sheaf of golden grain in his left arm, while his right holds a torch.

The Land of the Living Skies.

Golden Rails, Sunset over the Track. The golden rails in the setting sun symbolize the challenges which shaped the character and culture of the early pioneers who settled in the Canadian Midwest.

SASKATCHEWAN

Saskatchewan is a place steeped in the rich history and legends of aboriginal peoples. Evidence of their existence dates back to 10,000 B.C. Subsequently, many of the place names of our province originate from First Nations and Métis cultures.

The word "Saskatchewan" comes from the Cree Nation, a tribe which originally called the region "kisis-katchewan", meaning "swift-flowing river". There are three mighty rivers flowing through our province, including the Assiniboine, the South Saskatchewan, and the Churchill.

Although Saskatchewan is often associated with magnificent expanses of golden wheat fields, it is much more. One-third of the province is farmland, one-eighth is fresh water (with over 100,000 lakes comprising a total of 81,631 square kilometers), and a full half is forested. The hills in the southwest are 4,566 feet above sea level; we have two deserts - one featuring sand dunes up to thirty meters high (nowhere else in the

world are sand dunes found this far north), and our northern zone rests on a formation of Precambrian rock.

The beautiful land of the Prince Albert National park inspired English-born Archibald Belaney, better known as Grey Owl, to become one of the world's first naturalists in the 1930's. Grey Owl assumed an aboriginal identity and traveled extensively in England speaking eloquently about the importance of preserving the Canadian wilderness. Today, when enjoying a game of golf on the courses in this region, it is common to share the fairways with elk, bear, and other wildlife.

When I reflect on the natural beauty of my province, I am reminded of the writings of Saskatchewan author Sharon Butala, who has described the land of her birth as "a paradise of natural beauty, full of wild animals and birds, in winter, where the acres of snow and ice would catch the light and glow like burnished jewels, or where the fields of grass in

The Honorable Lynda Haverstock is Lieutenant Governor of Saskatchewan.

summer would record in moving shadows all the changes of the wild sky, and shimmer and bow and sing softly with every breeze".

Our people are defined by their relationship with the land, by the expansiveness of our sky, the kind of individualism that stems from surviving our strange dance with the elements, and the fact that in all of our 651,900 square kilometers, we number only one million residents. It is interesting to note that the entire United Kingdom is about one third the size of our province, with 55 times the population.

People from all over the world have settled here. Saskatchewan is the only province in Canada where the majority of the population is of neither British nor French background. Our province is comprised of people from many cultures, each contributing their own rich heritage and traditions.

Saskatchewan has one of the highest rates of voluntarism and charitable financial donations per capita in Canada. Voluntarism has a long, proud history in our province. Early settlers survived and flourished on this land, despite an unforgiving cli-

Prairie Lilies.

mate and challenging distances, by supporting each other and by planning with vision and foresight.

Our province has often been called the "bread basket" of the nation because it has been the country's largest producer of wheat. But Saskatchewan farmers are constantly diversifying. At the turn of the 21st century, Saskatchewan has 96% of Canada's seeded acreage of lentils and chickpeas, and many producers have diversified into canola, flax, sunflower and mustard, and even herbs and spices. Livestock production accounts for more than a quarter of our province's farm revenue, including beef, bison, elk and deer, horses, pork, poultry, sheep and goats, and wild boar, ostrich and lamas.

In addition to agriculture, Saskatchewan is rich in minerals, including uranium, coal, oil and natural gas. Furthermore, our province is the world's leading exporter of potash.

Saskatchewan is also on the forefront of scientific research. Researchers and scientists are developing one of the world's largest centres for plant biotechnology. Construction of one of Canada's largest scientific projects is underway at the University of Saskatchewan. The University was awarded the $174-million project to build a giant light source called the synchrotron. This 'field of beams' will enable scientists to observe living cells and atomic-scale matter. It could help them to discover new vaccines and medicines, develop disease-resistant plants, and examine patients without surgery.

If Saskatchewan is associated with vast expanses of wheat fields, we are also famous for our dramatic winters. With the cold, however, comes a stunning, quiet beauty as tree branches bow under the weight of heavy frost that glistens in the brilliant sunshine, our constant companion. At night, even though we have seen them many times, we continue to be held spellbound by the mystical sight of the aurora borealis. These magical northern lights are especially vivid away from the glare of the cities. And if our winters are cold, their intensity is matched by the warmth of the people who live under our magnificent skies.

I have had the great fortune of meeting thousands who call Saskatchewan home. I can promise anyone who visits this region of Canada a heartfelt smile and a welcoming embrace.

The Church of Saint Anthony of Padua in the Batoche National Historic Site is a moving tribute to the last stand of the métis in the North-West rebellion fought here in 1885. Despite the skill of the Métis cavalrymen and the young Cree allied with them, the rebellion was doomed when troops were rushed into the plains by the new railway line. Louis Riel, the great métis leader and founder of the Province of Manitoba, was captured, and put on trial. He was hanged in Regina in 1885.

History

Many of the great place names of Saskatchewan come from the First Nations and the métis people who once lived and hunted bison across the fertile plains of the prairie.

Three Athabaskan tribes lived in the north: the Chipewyan, the Beaver, and the Slavey. Two Algonquian tribes, the Cree and the Blackfoot, occupied the central part of the province. The south was inhabited largely by the Siouan tribes – the Assiniboine and the Gros Ventres.

Because much of the province was made up of prairie, it was of little monetary interest to the early fur traders, and southern Saskatchewan remained relatively untouched by Europeans for many years. The northern wooded regions, on the other hand, were dotted with fur-trading posts early in Canadian history.

The first explorer was Henry Kelsey, an employee of the Hudson's Bay Company, who followed the Saskatchewan river into the plains of Saskatchewan in 1690. Both Britain and the Province of Canada sent expeditions in the mid 1800's to explore the area and assess its agricultural potential.

In the early 1870's, the great Cree, Assiniboine, and Blackfoot confederacies still dominated the plains. For generations they had hunted the buffalo, which, at the time, darkened the prairies in vast numbers; it is estimated that over 60 million buffalo roamed the grasslands of North America. These enormous creatures were essential to the aboriginal people in many ways; from buffalo hides came their teepees and their clothing; their meat and their sinew thread for bow strings; their

Buffalo hunting on the prairies, Paul Kane.

fuel, cups, spoons, and ceremonial ornaments.

But by the 1870's the facts were clear. Eastern settlement pushed on inexorably, largely due to the fact that the Government of Canada had purchased the former Hudson's Bay holdings as a prelude to their incorporation in the Canadian Confederation. And as the great Canadian Pacific Railway snaked its way west, reaching completion in 1885, herds of buffalo were destroyed to clear the prairie for the ribbons of steel. Over that tragic period, many wise leaders of the aboriginal peoples, such as Maskepeooon of the Plains Cree, worked to ensure peace and unity among their people in a courageous struggle for survival.

But this was not to be. Even with the fine leadership of Crowfoot of the Blackfoot nation, the pressures of eastern settlement, epidemics, wars and the scarcity of the buffalo led to desperation and the subsequent signing of treaties with Canadian government agents. The Cree leader, Piapot, may have spoken for all in

declaring his eternal opposition "for as long as the rivers ran, as long as the grass grew, as long as men walked on two legs."

In 1870, the area that now makes up the province of Saskatchewan joined Confederation as part of the Northwest Territories. The Dominion Lands Act of 1872, combined with legislation to stimulate immigration, strongly encouraged homesteaders in Saskatchewan. In the 1880's, the newly constructed Canadian Pacific Railway brought settlers to farm the rich land. A great wave of immigration from Eastern Europe swept across the area in the late 19th and early 20th centuries.

In 1905, the Province of Saskatchewan was formed by joining the districts of Saskatchewan and parts of the districts of Athabaska and Assiniboia. It became the only province not based on any particular geographical features. Saskatchewan, and its neighboring province of Alberta also share the distinction of being the only Canadian provinces that are not bordered by salt water.

Although the photographers tend to concentrate on the magnificent expanses of golden wheatfields that seem to run on into eternity, fully one half the province is covered by forest, one-third is farmland and one-eighth is fresh water. (with over 100,000 lakes).

When the crops are ready for harvesting in the Province of Saskatchewan, grain farmers race against time to take advantage of the good weather.

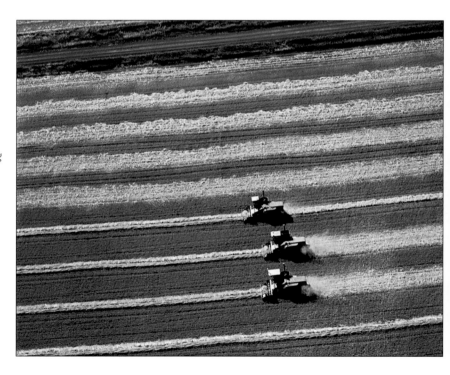

"On the prairie, one can see the colour of the air", said Emily C. Murphy, the first woman magistrate in the British Empire, now honored in Canada as a member of the Famous Five.

Diefenbaker Lake is the largest body of water in Southern Saskatchewan and was formed through the construction of two massive dams, the Qu'Appelle River dam and the Gardiner.

Aurora Borealis.

It is said that no river in Canada is like the wild and wonderful Saskatchewan section of the Churchill river. The upper part (the rest of the 1,000 mile river traverses northern Manitoba and empties into Hudson's Bay) is like an endless series of lakes connected by rapids and roaring waterfalls.

Saskatoon is known to many as Canada's most dynamic science city.

Legislative Building, Regina.

Wild Rose Country.
A Land of Shining Mountains. Love at First Sight!

Malak's famous photo of a cattle drive on the Canadian prairie in early spring has won many awards.

ALBERTA

The Honorable David Kilgour is Member of Parliament for Edmonton Southeast and Secretary of State for Asia and the Pacific.

It is always difficult to provide a short but adequate flavour to one's home province in the complex Canadian federation. This is particularly true with regard to Alberta, a country-sized area with seven distinct regions, and whose residents are of origin in virtually every member state of the United Nations.

Until recently, most of the world seemed to notice only our Rocky Mountains, rolling foothills, and glacier-fed rivers and lakes. Banff and Jasper National Parks are, of course, difficult for anyone, including other Canadians, to ignore when contemplating Alberta.

But what of the province's half dozen modern cities, of which Edmonton, our provincial capital and home to many festivals, and Calgary, the business head office magnet, compete in numerous fields? The fierce, yet fun-filled competition includes population growth (both metropolitan centres currently have approximately one million), cultural life (symphony orchestras, ballet, art, opera, theatre), universities and colleges, and sports. (track and field, hockey, football, soccer, basketball and baseball).

During the Calgary Stampede and Edmonton Klondike Days, thousands of volunteers dress in period costumes and relive earlier days to the delight of visitors and themselves. Yet it is the modern Albertans themselves who year round make the province the formidable national force it is today.

Out First Nations peoples probably arrived thousands of years ago from Asia and succeeded in establishing rich cultural and family lives in numerous communities, including the Blackfoot and Cree nations. Later in the late nineteenth century, when an estimated sixty million buffalo were slaughtered mostly for 'sport' by outsiders, their way of life disappeared and painful decades of adjustment began.

In the first decades of the twentieth century, pioneer families from almost everywhere on earth arrived in Prairie Canada (which was known as the last, best West) to break land for crops and to build local churches of many faiths and communities. In 1947, however, this settlement period changed substantively when oil was discovered near Edmonton. For example, the population of each province on the prairies then was about 750,000; today Alberta has slightly more than three times the population of each of our two sister provinces. (three million vs. one million).

Thousands of us work directly in the oil and gas sector, but far more earn livelihoods in related fields, such as pipeline construction and software design. The immense wealth created by oil ('black gold') and more recently by the relatively pollution-free natural gas, has allowed our schools and 29 or so post-secondary educational institutions to flourish. Our publicly-run health care system, highways and social programs are also among Canada's best. Many Albertans today know that abundant natural resources, unless handled with prudence and self-discipline can prove to be a curse.

I think the really fascinating feature of the province is our unique cultural mosaic, a consequence partly of the reality that no ethno-cultural group is numerically dominant. Members of every community, including the larger ones (English, German, Ukrainian, Scottish, Irish, First Nations, Chinese and French Canadian), believe that individuals are of equal worth and should have the freedom to choose their own lifestyle. A pattern of permissive differentiation in religion, language and culture, instead of assimilation, emerged quite early in the province. Following some bitter experiences with prejudice and discrimination, a truly international society with a habit of inclusiveness developed in Alberta.

The American Elk – The Shawnee Indians referred to this large deer (which can weigh up to 800 pounds) as waptiti or 'white rump.' It is the noisiest deer in Canada and during the mating season the males' bugle cry can carry for up to a mile.

Don't believe for a moment the "redneck" stereotype thrown so glibly at Albertans by some pundits. Many of our public schools, for instance, teach French from kindergarten to grade twelve; French immersion programs continue to attract many young Albertans. It is even possible to study only in French to the bachelor's level at the Faculte Saint Jean at the University of Alberta in Edmonton. There are also bilingual public school programs in Mandarin, Cree, Arabic, Ukrainian and German, among other languages.

One challenge that Alberta and the rest of Western Canada pose to other Canadians, is the adequacy of our present federal governance model. Most of our national institutions were essentially copied from those of Great Britain in place in 1867 when Canada was born, but today their democratic legitimacy is challenged, especially in the West. Many Albertans want them to be modernized so that residents of all five regions of our country will feel themselves to be politically, economically and culturally equal to their fellow Canadians.

Calgary Stampede, Calgary, Alberta.

Calgary's cowboy image is still very much part of the culture of this modern, vibrant city. But while the cattle industry is still important in Alberta, the modern skyline of the city attests to the fact that it is second in Canada only to Toronto in the number of corporate head offices. Only an hour from Calgary, the traveller finds little families such as those seen below.

This baby goat was probably born under a ledge high up in the Rocky Mountains of Alberta. The mother chose the ledge for protection from the golden eagles that regularly patrol the ridges looking for strays.

The moose and calf – The largest members of the deer family, the moose is a strong swimmer and they are often seen in northern lakes feeding on delicate water lilies.

The Alberta Badlands are a striking panorama of fluted gullies, the naturally sculpted pillars of rock and gravel known as hoodoos, and steep bluffs which were, between 64 and 140 million years ago, a sub-tropical lowland inhabited by dinosaurs.

History

Alberta was named for Queen Victoria's fourth daughter, Princess Louise Caroline Alberta, the wife of the Marquess of Lorne, who was Governor General of Canada in 1882.

The oldest identified archaeological sites in Alberta date back approximately 11,000 years. When Europeans reached what is now Alberta in the mid-18th century, the area was home to many different aboriginal nations.

In 1778, fur trader Peter Pond established the first fur trade post within the boundaries of modern Alberta. Soon other posts were constructed on the Athabasca, Peace and North Saskatchewan rivers by both the North West and Hudson's Bay companies.

In the mid-19th century, several scientific expeditions, most notably Captain John Palliser's expedition of 1857-1860, examined the agricultural potential of the Canadian west. Palliser believed that the southern prairies were too dry for farming. But further north, he and other observers, including the notable naturalist and geologist Henry Youle Hind, thought the land was fertile and well suited to agricultural settlement. In 1870, these lands, including most of present-day Alberta, were acquired by the Government of Canada.

Settlement was slow until the Canadian Pacific Railway reached Alberta in 1883. The railway made it easier for new settlers to get to Alberta and to sell the crops they grew. In 1891, a railway was completed from Calgary to Strathcona, across the North Saskatchewan River from Edmonton. Other railway lines followed, including the transcontinental Grand Trunk Pacific and Canadian Northern railways, which reached Edmonton in 1911.

In 1905, Alberta and its neighbour, Saskatchewan, entered Confederation. For the first time, the Canadian provinces were joined from sea to sea. Settlement boomed in Alberta. Land in the new province was readily available at low cost under the Homestead Act, or could be purchased from railway and other land companies. The discovery of new strains of wheat and other grains suited to western Canadian growing conditions and new methods of farming also helped encourage rapid settlement.

In ten years, the population increased over five times to 374,000.

Subsequently, it increased substantially to more than 584,000 in 1921. As a result, the population of Alberta came to be made up of many people of different backgrounds, languages, and cultures.

Alberta's destiny was changed forever in 1947, when a major oil discovery was made at Leduc, near Edmonton. As more and more oil and gas discoveries were made, a share of the oil money flowed to the provincial government.

Jobs were created in the petrochemical industry, as well as in construction, surveying, and transportation. Edmonton and Calgary emerged as prosperous cities of business and finance, surpassing their rural neighbours.

After World War II, immigrants continued to come to Alberta from different parts of the world, including Asia and the Caribbean.

While Alberta's economy has continued to expand in many areas, oil still plays a large role in its prosperity. When the price of oil is high, Alberta prospers. When it drops, as it did in the mid-1980s, times may be difficult. In the 1990s, improved oil prices and the growth of new industries helped make Alberta's economy one of the strongest in Canada. Worldwide, Alberta is the 18th largest producer, the second largest natural gas exporter, and in 1998 accounted for 69% of all the energy produced in Canada. Alberta's oil sands reserves contain an estimated 1.7 trillion barrels of bitumen in place.

Train through the Rockies.

Oil rig backed by mountains.

The old Prince of Wales Hotel overlooks Waterton-Glacier International Peace Park, Alberta. Occupied for thousands of years by the Blackfoot tribe, this 'land of shining mountains' is a sanctuary for huge old spruce and fir and some of Canada's most interesting wildlife.

The Banff-Jasper Highway provides travellers with one of the most visually breathtaking panoramas on earth. Adjoining Banff National Park at the Columbia Icefield, Jasper Park sweeps northwest along the continental divide that separates Alberta and British Columbia.

Edmonton is the capital of Alberta. It is a vibrant metropolis which has, from its beginnings as the most important fur trading post in the West, been a vital gateway to the north. The impressive Legislative Building, is set in pleasant gardens overlooking the North Saskatchewan river.

Beautiful, Bountiful, Heaven Blessed.

Malahat Drive, Vancouver Island.

BRITISH COLUMBIA

From its majestic snow-capped Rockies, roaring rivers and pristine lakes, to the dry, hot heat of summer in the semi-arid tree-fruit and grape-growing interior. To its endless blue skies, sun-drenched prairies, sweeping wheat fields and glaciers in the far north. To cowboy country, the central cattle plains and the lush agricultural valleys in the south.

To the mighty Pacific – its tides, storms, fierce gales and balmy off-shore breezes. All the picturesque islands, harbours and plentiful harvests from an abundant sea. Yes, and the trees. Everywhere the trees – the friendly cedar, enormous fir, pungent pine and stately oak. The soaring eagles, seagulls, songbirds and wild animals of the forests and glens.

Each region different. Each region unique. Each one a marvel of its own. And, thanks to the warm Japanese currents, enjoying Canada's most friendly and temperate climate.

And riches: One-third of all of Canada's fresh water flow. Enormous natural energy capacities, no end still untapped – hydroelectric, gas, oil and coal. World's largest softwood exporter – 60% of Canada's lumber, 30% of its pulp. Plus every mineral one can think of – 40% of Canada's lead and 41% of its copper. Possessing a trained, skilled workplace, Canada's Gateway to the enormous markets of the Pacific Rim, and our country's best entry into Free-Trade North America.

For no longer does British Columbia just cut, catch, dig, pick, pump and ship. For firmly entrenched is the new breed – the leading-edge know-how, the high-tech and value-added – globally competing, and, globally succeeding. Everywhere bright, brand new facilities. Up-to-the-minute trans-

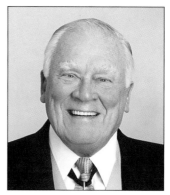

The Honorable Garde B. Gardom, Q.C. is the former lieutenant governor of British Columbia.

portation links – rail, road, ferry, plane and sea. Great emphasis on family life, on home ownership and unspoiled nature at its best.

Also a rich history – that of our first citizens, our Native Indian communities, and their living cultures, of our European explorers, the British, Spanish and Russian, and our rugged pioneers and early settlers.

But most of all our people – of every race, religion, colour and creed. Go-getters, entrepreneurs, but also ensuring Volunteerism is always a way of life. Caring. Sharing. Helping. Doing unto others. Enjoying education and health the envy of many. Plus the excitement of the cities: Vibrant, up-beat, cosmopolitan Vancouver. Canada's largest port – deep-sea, year-round. Plus quaint, gorgeous-gardened, laid-back Victoria – Canada's "Springtime" choice.

British Columbia – energetic, thriving, peaceful. A tourism destination without parallel. Fresh air. Clear water. Fertile soil. Remarkable scenery. Recreational activities everywhere – attainable and affordable. Yes, a quality of life bar none, and with lots of room for lots of people with lots of opportunity.

Heaven-blessed? I'll say!

Roberta Bondar wrote: "The greens and browns of this exposed sea life in Gwaii Haanas National Park Reserve caught my eye at low tide. Clouds bring fresh water to trees and plants that live on islands surrounded by salt water. Rain is recycled to the sea whose ebb and flow revitalizes communities of rich ocean life."

The indigenous people of the northwest coast enjoyed a high standard of living and had the leisure time to carve tall tree trunks with expressive forms and symbols, which were often works of art, but also functional means of identification of families and clans or as memorials to dead relatives. The totem poles represent an art form unique to the westcoast First Nations.

The lovely copper domes of the Parliament Buildings tower over Victoria's Inner Harbour. Victoria is the capital of British Columbia and is famous for its 'high teas', its beautiful gardens, and it's elegance and gentility. Canadian author Stephen Leacock once wrote of Victoria: "If I had known of this place before, I would have been born here."

Campbell River area – salmon seiners in Johnstone Strait, British Columbia.

Butchart Gardens are now internationally famous, but were originally conceived by Jenny Butchart, wife of a quarry owner, to beautify the pit. Now more than a million plants delight visitors on Vancouver Island's Saanich Peninsula. The Waterfall of Lights at Christmas is made up of over 500,000 bulbs.

Canada's third largest metropolis, Vancouver is almost entirely surrounded by a treasure-house of mountains. Despite heavy snowfall that provides almost perfect skiing in the region, Vancouver rarely receives snow. A protected deep sea port with accessibility to the Pacific, Vancouver is a wonderful combination of modern highrises and great natural beauty.

History

Unlike Eastern Canada, where the French and English disputed control of the land, the first two countries to contest areas of British Columbia were Spain and Russia. In the 1700s, the Spanish claimed ownership of the west coast of North America from Mexico to Vancouver island. At the same time, the Russians were making an overlapping claim: control of the Pacific coast from Alaska to San Francisco.

In 1778, Captain James Cook of Great Britain became the first person to actually chart the land. George Vancouver, a 20-year-old midshipman on Cook's voyage, later led three expeditions of his own and charted more than 16,000 kilometres of coastline.

His description of the area around Vancouver would be apparent to all modern enthusiasts of this most beautiful of regions. "To describe the beauties of this region will, on some future occasion, be a very grateful task to the pen of a skilled panegyrist. The serenity of the climate, the innumerable pleasing landscapes, and the abundant fertility that unassisted nature puts forth, requires only to be enriched by the industry of man... to render it the most lovely country that can be imagined." (*Spring of 1792, A Voyage of Discovery to the North Pacific Ocean and Round the World*).

In June, 1793, Captain Vancouver's boat crews explored an inlet near Bella Coola. If they had stayed a little longer, they would have made a rendevous with Alexander MacKenzie, whose single canoe carried himself and nine men all the way to British Columbia – with intermittent portages – from Montreal. To reach the Pacific, they had to leave the canoe and walk through the mountains to the sea. He left his name and the date of his arrival in a mixture of fish grease and red dye at Bella Coola; a wonderful place where lush forest surrounds roaring rivers. Today his words are carved and painted as a permanent memorial to his remarkable journey.

David Thompson did not complete single feats of exploration such as Alexander Mackenzie and Simon Fraser. But he did explore the mountain labyrinths of British Columbia for years as a mapmaker and as a master of geographical surveying. Thompson died in 1857, old, blind, and forgotten, but was remembered by generations after for his essential role in mapping the vast territory from Lake Superior to the Pacific. Today, photographers capture the thrill of whitewater rafting down the Thompson river named after this solitary hero.

Over the intervening decades, having firmly established her right to the area, Britain proceeded to settle disputes with both Spain and Russia. The 1846 Oregon Treaty with the United States gave Britain the ownership of Vancouver island and the area north of the 49th parallel. In 1849, Vancouver island was granted to the Hudson's Bay Company in the hope that it might be settled. Until that time, the only European settlements in that part of the country were fur-trading posts.

When gold was discovered in the lower Fraser Valley in 1857, thousands of people came in search for instant wealth. To help maintain law and order, the British government established the separate colony of British Columbia the following year. The southern part of the area now

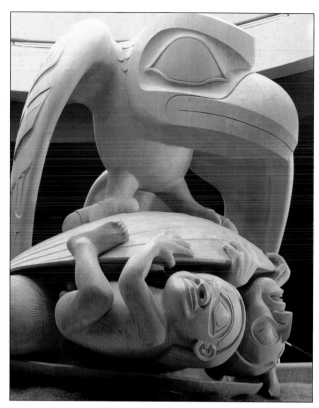

The Raven and the First Men at the University of British Columbia Museum of Anthropology, Vancouver, B.C., was carved from a 4 1/2 ton block of 106 beams of yellow cedar – laminated together and unveiled in 1980. Sculptors Gary Edenshaw, George Morris, and George Hammel all participated with the internationally known Haida sculptor Bill Reid.

tribes of any province or territory in Canada. First Nations people have lived in the area for more than 7,000 years. Because of the diversity of the Pacific coast – mild to cold climates, seashore to mountain tops - the tribes that settled in this area developed completely different cultures and languages. They were not only different from each other, but also from the rest of the Indian tribes in Canada.

On the misty Queen Charlotte islands lies the homeland of the great Haida nation. Their war canoes once cut through the waters of the Pacific Northwest. In all of their villages, which were comprised of large houses made of cedar planks, stood forests of totem poles. Most of the Haida villages were abandoned in the late 1800's. But one of their sayings is very significant for mankind as we enter into this new century. 'We do not inherit the land from our forefathers, we borrow it from our children.'

known as British Columbia was called Columbia, after the Columbia river, and the central region was given the name of New Caledonia by explorer Simon Fraser. To avoid confusion with Columbia in South America, Queen Victoria named the area British Columbia when it became a colony in 1858.

In 1866, when the frenzy of the gold rush was over, the colony of Vancouver Island joined the colony of British Columbia.

British Columbia was separated from the rest of British North America by thousands of kilometres and the imposing Rocky Mountains. But the promise of a rail link from the Pacific coast to the rest of Canada convinced the colony to join Confederation in 1871.

The province was inhabited by the greatest number of distinct Indian

A replica of a Haida canoe at the Museum of Civilization in Ottawa.

Rain Forest, British Columbia.

The lengthy coastline of British Columbia is a fascinating blend of alluring, rugged cliffs, forest-clad peaks, winding, twisting waterways, an enormous variety of islands, bays and fjords, as well as restless surf and sandy beaches. In the background, there are always the towering mountains, often rising in places to 6,000 feet.

Along the misty, moody coastline is the dark, damp rainforest of ancient fir, cedar, and hemlock. The aboriginal people who lived in this enchant-ed land of forest, mountain peaks, deep canyons, and ocean were known as the people of the salmon. For thousands of years before the arrival of the Europeans, they harpooned and net-ted shimmering hoards of the sacred fish as they continued their incredi-ble odyssey upstream to spawn. The salmon had a deep spiritual signifi-cance to the distinctive tribes of the region.

A rare Kermode Bear or Spirit Bear capturing a salmon on Princess Royal Island on the British Columbia coast.

Whistler is a world renowned ski resort.

Horseshoe Bay, Howe Sound, British Columbia.

One of the jewels in the diadem of mountains near Whistler glows in the moonlight.

Little Qualicum Falls, on Vancouver Island, flows from a lake high on a mountain in British Columbia.

The Magic and the Mystery.

Evening, as the moon rises over the mountains, can be one of the most beautiful times in the Yukon. For all of those who experience the grandeur of Canada's Yukon Territory – beware. This remarkable region – which is the size of Sweden – has a way of making the visitor her's forever.

THE YUKON TERRITORY

"... Dreaming of men who will bless me, of women esteeming me good,
Of children born in my borders of radiant motherhood.
Of cities leaping to stature, of fame like a flag unfurled,
As I pour the tide of my riches in the eager lap of the world

The Law of the Yukon – Robert Service

The Honorable Sue Edelman.
Minister of Health, former Minister of
Tourism.

Approximately five hundred and fifty years ago, before Columbus set foot on the east coast, a man who has come to be known as Kwaday Dän Sinchi, or Long Ago Person Found, lost his life while walking a trade route between what is now Alaska and the Yukon. Recently laid to his eternal rest by his descendants with the ceremonies prescribed by ageless customs, this gentleman provides a stark reminder of the occupation of a region that dates back thousands of years.

What is now the Yukon Territory was once a part of the transportation route used by wildlife and people as they crossed through Beringia from Europe and populated North America. Animals that are now extinct such as the woolly mammoth, the sabre cat and the giant sloth once roamed this land as the ice ages advanced and retreated. The people also moved further south, following their food sources, and in turn established their presence as far as South America.

Just over one hundred years ago, the Yukon became a focal point for the world as tens of thousands of people abandoned their lives on the farms and in the cities and flooded into the Klondike to search for gold. At the height of the Gold Rush, Dawson City was the largest city west of Winnipeg and north of San Francisco. The great Klondike Gold Rush established the romantic and economic future of the Yukon. The majority of the people left after the rush, but some stayed to build a life and create the communities that are with us still.

Much of our recent history focuses on the tribulations and hardships of the prospectors in their search for wealth. Until recently, little was mentioned of the tremendous impacts to Yukon's first nation people as a result of the influx of settlers from other places.

The prospectors brought diseases, alcohol, modem commerce and an alien culture to the Klondike that had a profound impact on the life-style of the aboriginal people. The aboriginal people were ignored in their protests by the governments responsible as they were focused at the time on the flood of immigrants to the region and the need to determine the formal borders between Canada and the United States.

Today, Yukon first nation people are gaining back their rights to their traditional lands through a land claims process that has been underway since the late 1970's. Economic opportunities, resources and self-governance are the critical elements of today's agreements. In many respects we are learning how to rebuild our society as we move ahead with the land claims process.

The Yukon's first nations people are creating their own futures through these modern self government agreements. Their decisions and values reflect their view of how they wish to advance into the future. Their future includes much of their past where traditional practices and knowledge are being rediscovered and taught to their children. In this way they will maintain a connection to their cultural history and their language which makes them unique in the world.

The pristine wilderness of the Yukon is drawing people from around the world. During the summer months when the sun is reluctant to set, clear rivers and lakes, picturesque mountain ranges and vast unpopulated areas beckon travellers to the Yukon. They are also coming in the winter months to experience the snow, the cold weather and the captivating beauty of the Aurora Borealis as made famous by the writings of Robert Service and Jack London.

Numerous stories have been written about life in the Yukon as the last frontier and a place of incredible

The Dog Sled Race – Dog teams take off in Whitehorse, the start of a 1,800 kilometre Yukon Quest race to Fairbanks, Alaska.

beauty and harshness. While modern creature comforts such as electricity and Internet communications are now serving the Yukon's communities, it is a short walk out the back door to be surrounded by the wilderness experience.

People here live with nature on their doorsteps and appreciate the small town atmosphere in the majority of our communities. As with most small towns, Yukoners are active in many capacities to ensure a healthy lifestyle. Volunteerism is outstanding as many community-based activities flourish around sports, the arts and improving their community.

The Yukon's population is approximately thirty thousand people scattered throughout a landmass about the size of Sweden. The majority of Yukon towns are located next to a waterway as these were the primary transportation routes used during the Gold Rush.

An astounding accomplishment, even by today's standards, was the creation of the Whitepass and Yukon Route Railway that runs from Skagway Alaska. It was built over the high mountain peaks of the pacific coast and terminated in Whitehorse. Built by hand through vertical slopes of rock and over deep treacherous ravines, the railway is a testament to the fortitude and endurance of those early gold-seekers. The train still runs today, giving visitors a first hand view of the beauty and danger in this unforgiving land.

During World War II, the Alaska Highway was built from northern British Columbia, through the Yukon to central Alaska to ensure a land route from the northern reaches of the continent to the populated centres in the south. No small feat, the nearly fifteen hundred-mile highway was completed in just over a year.

A network of highways now connects all Yukon communities with the exception of Old Crow, our most northerly community. The highway network has allowed the communities to grow and become greater participants in the Yukon economy.

Many Yukon communities had their beginnings in the early fur trade or the Gold Rush. Some were created to support the mining operations that developed nearby. While mining activity is not as prominent as it once was, many communities are now expanding their tourism attractions to be gateways to the wilderness features in their area.

Still a relatively young part of Canada, the Yukon is old, measured in other terms. Our history and culture is rich and diverse. The warmth of our people offsets the cold of the winter weather. As you have probably determined, I can go on and on about this wonderful land, but to really appreciate it, you have to see it for yourself

Consider a visit to the fabled land of the midnight sun. The people will welcome you with genuine hospitality and Mother Nature will display her beauty as you have never seen.

History

The Yukon territory's name comes from the native name word "Yu-kunah" meaning great river. In 1846, chief trader John Bell of the Hudson's Bay Company canoed down the Porcupine River to its confluence with the Yukon River, where he met natives who told him that the name of the big river was the "youcon". The Yukon River is the fifth longest in North America.

Yukon was probably the first area in Canada to be settled, following the migration of the ancestors of First Nations across the Bering Strait land bridge from Asia to North America some 4,000 years ago.

Language is central to Yukon First Nation heritage. The history and traditions of the many Yukon First Nations have been passed down through the generations orally by the teachings of elders. There are seven Athapaskan languages spoken in Yukon.

In 1825, John Franklin became the first European to reach Yukon, then part of Rupert's Land, when he followed the Arctic coastline in search of the Northwest Passage. By 1848,

Robert Service's cabin with actor reading his poetry.

the Hudson's Bay Company had established four trading posts on a traditional First Nation trading route.

In 1870, the Government of Canada acquired the territory from the Hudson's Bay Company and the entire region became known as the Northwest Territories. The bound-

aries of Yukon were first drawn in 1895, when it became a district of the Northwest Territories. Because of its remote location and severe climate, Yukon's population remained sparse until the discovery of gold.

In 1896, three prospectors found gold at Rabbit Creek, 'lying thick between the flaky slabs of rock like cheese in a sandwich.' After that, thousands of hopeful goldseekers headed north. Some went to Edmonton and took the lengthy route overland to the North. Most hopefuls sailed to Skagway, Alaska and took the fearful Trail of 98.

Dawson City, at the junction of the Klondike and Yukon rivers, was at the time, home to 40,000 people. The vast majority of prospectors, dance hall girls, hotelkeepers, and gamblers left Yukon poorer than when they arrived. But a young bank clerk named Robert Service did get rich by writing about

Can-can girls recreate the raucous atmosphere of the Klondike gold rush. Names like Mollie Fewclothes and Ethel the Moose were all part of the colour of the heyday of some of the biggest, richest mining towns like Dawson.

Indian Paint Brush, sometimes called Purple Fireweed, the offficial floral emblem of the Yukon, wave in beauty beneath a summer sky.

depleted the population dropped dramatically.

When Yukon became a separate territory, the Yukon Act of 1898 provided for a Commissioner and a legislative council of six, all appointed by the Government of Canada.

Nearly a century later, in 1979, an Executive Committee was established to assist the Territorial Commissioner in the executive function. The elected members of the Executive Committee have progressively assumed greater responsibilities.

With the formal introduction of party politics in 1978, the elected leader of the majority party in the legislature became known as the Government Leader. When responsible government was established in 1979, the Commissioner no longer participated in the Executive Council. The Government Leader, or Premier, has the authority to determine the size and the appointments to the Executive Council, paralleling the function of the premiers in the provinces.

the gold lust. His poems about 'the strange things done in the midnight sun by the men who toil for gold' made him famous all around the world.

Between 1896 and 1903, more than $95 million in gold was mined from the Klondike region. But once the easily extracted placer gold was

Set on a dramatic site on the east bank of the wide Yukon river at the confluence with the Klondike, Dawson is an historic frontier town which is like a Western movie set and is still a major tourist attraction in Yukon. August 17, 'Discovery Day', is an annual holiday replete with parades and raft races on the Yukon.

Kluane National Park is Canada's second largest national park with an astonishing variety of sights to stagger the imagination. Here we see the Kaskowalsh Glacier, a river of ice spread across a valley floor.

The Klondike River Valley is a mass of gravel tailings left by gigantic dredges that stripped river bottoms down to bedrock in search of gold.

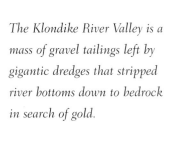

The Alaska Highway connects Dawson Creek, British Columbia, with Fairbanks, Alaska. It is an all-season highway, traversing one of the most scenic areas of North America.

Tombstone Mountains.

Marsh Lake, just south of Whitehorse, is a spring staging area for Trumpeter Swans and other waterfowl searching for open water in the Arctic. The first birds usually arrive in March.

The summer-no sweeter was ever;
The sunshiny woods all athrill;
The grayling aleap in the river,
The bighorn asleep on the hill.
The strong life that never knows harness;
The wilds where the caribou call;
The freshness, the freedom, the farness –
O God! How I'm stuck on it all.

(*The Spell of the Yukon, Robert Service*)

Is Heaven more Beautiful than the Country of the Muskox?
Where the Water is Blue and the Loons cry very often.
(Inuit saying)

South Nahanni River.

THE NORTHWEST TERRITORIES

Northwest Territories

The Northwest Territories is a vast land covering 1.17 million square kilometres of visually stunning mountains, forest, tundra, and clean rivers. There are countless lakes, abundant wildlife, rich cultural traditions, extraordinary people and world class fishing and hunting. Nature is in balance in the Northwest Territories. Rare wildlife species found here include white wolves, white whales, wood bison, whooping cranes, grizzly bears, and caribou. The world's most spectacular light show, the Aurora Borealis, dances across Northwest Territories skies during the fall and winter months. Located in Canada's north, the Northwest Territories is nestled in between the two other territories - Yukon to the west and Nunavut to the east.

Attractions include four national parks — Wood Buffalo, Nahanni, Tuktut Nogait and Aulavik. A few of the world-renowned wonders of the Northwest Territories include Virginia Falls, which is located in the Nahanni and is twice the height of Niagara Falls, the frozen pingos of Tuktoyaktuk and the Salt Flats of Wood Buffalo National Park. Canoeing or rafting legendary rivers like the Nahanni, cruising on the mighty Mackenzie River, and fishing for world record trophy fish on Great Bear or Great Slave Lake, which are some of the largest lakes in North America, are just a few of the adventures the Northwest Territories is famous for.

Our residents are a unique blend of Aboriginal people (Dene, Metis, and Inuvialuit) and non-aboriginal. With a total population of only 41,000, a visitor to a community is quickly recognized and warmly welcomed. Our 33 communities range in size from the capital city of Yellowknife with a population of 18,000 to the small traditional Dene community of Nahanni Butte with 76 people. Other regional centres in the Northwest Territories include Inuvik, Norman Wells, Fort Simpson, Hay River and Fort Smith.

The first inhabitants of the Northwest Territories were the Dene, who consist of Chipewyan, Dogrib, Yellowknives, Slavey, Gwich'in, Sahtu Dene and Cree. Their traditional homelands are the forested areas along the Mackenzie River and Great Slave and Great Bear Lakes.

The Inuvialuit, whose ancestors include the Inupiat of Alaska and Inuit of Nunavut, moved into the northern part of the NWT several hundred years ago. The homeland of the Inuvialuit stretches from the Alaskan border east to Amundsen Gulf and the western edge of the Canadian Arctic Islands.

The Metis, who were mainly descendants of French or French-Canadian men and Dene women, worked as canoe men and packers for the Hudson's Bay and Northwest Companies in the late 1700's and early 1800's.

The traditions and cultures of the Dene, Inuvialuit and Metis are still very much alive and reflected in all

The Honorable Joseph L. Handley, Minister of Finance, Government House Leader.

aspects of community life. Aboriginal people make up about half of the population.

Explorers and fur traders travelled to the NWT in the 18th and early 19th centuries to establish fur trading posts and forts for either the Hudson's Bay Company or the North West Company. Some of these early explorers included Samuel Hearne, Sir Alexander Mackenzie and Sir John Franklin. This history is alive in our Elders who can recount the tales of how their grandparents and great grandparents helped these explorers travel and survive in this great land. Permanent settlements were established near some of these forts and along main transportation routes. Another influx of people into the Northwest Territories came in the 1930's with mineral development, particularly gold and uranium mining. The transfer of government responsibilities from Ottawa to Yellowknife in the 1960's brought more people to the NWT.

The Northwest Territories is entering an exciting new era of economic potential that is capturing interest on a worldwide scale. Leading the way in this new economy is the diverse combination of oil and gas, diamonds and tourism. All three sectors can be classified as having world-class potential that is relatively untapped.

In 1991, the first diamonds were discovered in the Northwest Territories. Since then, the NWT has become the centre of the diamond industry in North America. Currently, there is one operating mine, BHP's Ekati Mine. The second mine, Diavik Diamond Mines will begin production in 2003 as well as a third property, owned by DeBeers.

Together, these mines are expected to produce gross revenues estimated at over $26 billion dollars. NWT diamonds are becoming recognized and sought after for their exceptional clarity and brilliance, and, with the establishment of a diamond sorting and valuation facility and three cutting and polishing plants, are creating employment and new careers for Aboriginal residents.

In the Northwest Territories, the people of Canada's First Nations make up about 50% of the population.

Renewed interest in the NWT's oil and gas sector has steadily increased over the last few years. Increased worldwide demand for energy products, high prices and depleting southern reserves, are paving the way for northern petroleum supplies.

The Northwest Territories is on the brink of being a major North American energy supplier within the next decade. A Mackenzie Valley gas pipeline could link the three major areas of oil and gas activity – the Deh Cho, Beaufort/Delta and Sahtu regions – to move natural gas from the Arctic Ocean to northern communities and southern markets.

Whether it is our multi-cultural heritage, diamonds, oil and gas or the Aurora Borealis, the Northwest Territories has international appeal to investors and tourists alike. It's a very exciting time to live in the Northwest Territories and I invite you to visit us soon.

Muskox on Tundra: The Northwest Territories is among the world's last great wildlife refuges. Large game animals still roam free: moose browse forest ponds, Dall's sheep climb craggy slopes and wood bison roam the grasslands. The prehistoric muskox which lives on the tundra is one of the largest of these.

Virginia Falls – The Nahanni River's Niagara Falls (in reality, twice the height of Niagara) is Virginia Falls. As the lower part of the river flows through Nahanni National Park, it thunders over Virginia Falls in a cataract that attracts photographers from all over the world.

The astonishing delicacy of Arctic flowers which spring from vast regions of snow and ice provide an array of brilliant colours.

The wilderness parks of the Northwest Territories capture the essence of the North. Wood Buffalo National Park is a subarctic of spectacular size and variety, where Canada's largest free-roaming bisons graze, and whooping cranes nest.

Yellowknife, capital of the Northwest Territories, is almost completely surrounded by water and sits on the northern shore of the Great Slave Lake. The igloo shaped Legislative Assembly Building is a lovely reflection of the Northern Heritage of the Territories, in particular of the Inuvialuit, whose ancestors include the Inupiat of Alaska and Inuit of Nunavut.

The North Nahanni River is a wilderness river recognized around the world as one of Canada's treasures.

Great Slave Lake, one of the largest and deepest lakes in the world, is a an inland sea of sparkling fresh water. In summer, avid fishermen of all ages try their hand at catching trophy size trout, kingsize Northern pike, and ruby red Arctic char.

This black bear sitting happily in a riotous glen of flowers is actually up to very serious business. The short sighted black bear is primarily vegetarian and up to 75% of his diet is made up of berries, flowers, grasses, tubers, nuts, and the like.

As one studies his photo, one can almost hear the voice of Grey Owl:

"Remember
you belong to Nature
not it to you."

(Grey Owl Nature Trust)

White Pelicans.

Falcons soar the river canyons. Birdwatchers flock to the Northern regions to see the vast migrations that converge on Arctic nesting grounds each summer.

> *"We are no longer dreaming.*
> *This is reality.*
> *We have arrived."*
> (*Premier Paul Okalik on the creation of Nunavut, April 1, 1999*)

This Inuit mother and her baby represent the future of Nunavut, Canada's newest territory. The 27,00 people, 85 percent Inuit and, with 56 percent under 25 years of age, the youngest population in Canada, are scattered in 26 communities, most, vast distances apart.

Auyuittuq National Park.

NUNAVUT

April 1, 1999. A day of joy and celebration. This was the day the territory of Nunavut was created in Canada's Eastern Arctic.

For the Inuit of Nunavut April 1, 1999 was the realization of a dream after more than three decades of peaceful negotiation. It was a day of creation, a day of renewal, a day of hope. It was a day of pride not only in Nunavut, but also across Canada and in many other areas of the world. We are proud of this achievement, for we in Canada have demonstrated what can be accomplished through dedication, hard work and patience.

The creation of the territory of Nunavut is a laudable example of tenacity and understanding. The development of Nunavut and the reclaiming of the Inuit homeland is a testament that through embracing diversity and change, a nation grows stronger, not weaker.

Geographically, Nunavut is immense – one-fifth the size of Canada – stretching across nearly two million square kilometres of land, water and ice. Nunavut has a sparse population, however, with an estimated 27,000 residents making their homes in 26 small communities spread throughout the territory. An estimated 85 per cent of these residents are Inuit.

Nunavut's capital, Iqaluit, is located

Boys playing at Pangnirtung.

on Baffin Island. Once known as Frobisher Bay, named after explorer Martin Frobisher, the City has a population approaching 6,000, and growing.

Iqaluit has been compared to some of the frontier towns of the 19th Century, and one could go so far as to say that the North is Canada's frontier for the 21st Century, especially in light of the enormous potential for renewable and non-renewable resource development.

For centuries, Inuit life passed virtually undisturbed by the outside world. However, European whalers and explorers first began travelling to Canada's North several hundred years ago. What they discovered along the Arctic coasts were small, nomadic communities of Inuit following the migration routes of various animal herds.

To this day, Inuit, predominantly a maritime people, depend largely on marine mammals, such as seal, walrus and whale, for their daily nourishment. Caribou also makes up a substantial part of the Inuit diet.

It was only a brief 50 years ago that life for the Inuit of Nunavut changed dramatically. Inuit relocated from igloos and summer tents to permanent houses in fixed communities. The transition from land-based lives to community-based living, resulted in cultural upheaval for Inuit. As our Elders can attest, Nunavut has seen tremendous change in this century.

When the Nunavut Land Claims Agreement – the largest in Canadian history – was signed in 1993, it represented approximately 18,000 Inuit and covered nearly two million square kilometres. The Agreement included title to 318,000 square kilometres of surface land rights and approximately

The Honorable Paul Okalik is Premier of Nunavut.

38,000 square kilometres of subsurface land rights for oil, gas and minerals. That represents 18 per cent of the total land area of Nunavut. In exchange for surrendering aboriginal title to land in Nunavut, Inuit received constitutionally protected rights to land, money, renewable resources, and social and political development.

Inuit accomplished a form of self-government that manifests itself within a public government structure. In the election of the first Nunavut Legislative Assembly in February, 1999 the residents of Nunavut, collectively called Nunavummiut, elected 19 representatives.

Since the creation of Nunavut, Nunavummiut have endeavoured to incorporate traditional Inuit values and customs – Inuit Qaujimajatuqangit – into every fibre of life in the territory. Nunavummiut are working to establish the conditions under which they may begin to change their lives in a meaningful way.

This will take time, but the indomitable spirit and resolve that saw Inuit through centuries of a harsh Arctic climate, only to flourish with a culture rich and diverse, will see that determination and tenacity achieve success in this century as well.

Auyuittuq National Park – Nunavut includes seven of Canada's twelve largest islands and one of these is Baffin Island, in itself two times the size of Great Britain.

The polar bear is one of the largest land animals in Canada, weighing up to 1,600 pounds. Polar bears frequent the arctic coast and, in winter, spend their time hunting seals and walrus. They have excellent eye-sight and are very strong swimmers.

Canadian Coast Guard in Eureka Sound with Ellesmere Island in the distance.

Most islands of the High Arctic are surrounded by frozen sea year-round; ice permanently covers large areas of both land and sea and the winters are fierce. The largest ice caps are found on Ellesmere Island, where they can be more than a kilometre thick and may cover more than 20,000 km.

Sunset over Ice Flow at Eureka Sound.

"In any of Nunavut's 26 communities, it is possible to walk for half an hour in any direction and find yourself beyond telephone poles, traffic and other trappings of civilization. And every step further on spongy tundra or snow swept ground increases the chances that no one has stepped where you are stepping.

As a newspaper reporter for three years in Iqaluit, I found in Nunavut's landscape, wildlife and sky, ceaseless novelty. Wearing a parka nine months of the year and buying wool socks by the bushel was no great chore for the wonders I found: making tea with chunks of icebergs, building igloos beneath impossible aurora and watching endless sunsets meld into slow sunrises.

But it was in the Inuit where I found the most insight – the elders and the children, the soapstone carvers and the politicians, the exalted hunters and the destitute.

My friend Paul Irngaut and I used to take long trips on water and ice. We stopped often so he could turn around and study the landscape we were leaving behind. You had to know what was behind you, he said, because that's what you see on the way back. When the land sprawled out featureless, we built Inuksuit to guide us home.

For a quarter century, Inuit leaders wrangled with Ottawa negotiators, desperate to lasso a land claim before missionaries and mercenaries forever changed their northern home. Many stumbled under the weight of that leadership, but most managed to pass on the wisdom of success and failure.

For generations, they thrived in a land few dared even to visit. Today they face their biggest challenge yet; self-government and public administration. Elected officials vow to promote hunting, support elders, teach Inuktitut in school and hire Inuit ahead of others. But it all costs money, and they are a small population on a giant, unruly land that is thawing and warming under climate change.

Nunavut, Our Land in Inuktitut, is made of rocks, bones and wind. A semi-arid desert, it has no trees and precious little greenery to offer guests. Its long, teeth rattling winters keep all but the hardiest wanderers from its fiords and hills.

Lisa Gregoire is a journalist with the Edmonton Journal whose reminiscences of Nunavut spark the reader to discover the majesty of the place.

But it is not bereft of beauty. It just takes more work to find it. Like the Inuit, Nunavut's charm is quiet and dignified, slow to reveal itself. It hovers near your feet when the sinking sun turns the snow pink-orange. It struggles inside tiny wild flowers on the land. It simmers in the caribou stew and rings from the drum dancer's song. It emerges in the eyes of seals, in the wings of ravens and in the heavy sighs of tired sled dogs before slumber."

Beautifully sculptured icebergs march into Cumberland Sound, where in summer they enhance the blue of the sea, the gray of the cliffs.

Iqualuit, the capital of Nunavut is located on Baffin Island. Once known as Frobisher Bay (named after explorer Martin Frobisher) the City has a population approaching 6,000.

Oliver Sound.

The famous Inuit soapstone and ivory carvings in particular are known for the stories they tell or the social conditions they depict. Most art from this region is founded in traditional lifestyles, animals, shamans, spirits and mythologies. Print making and wall hangings are also popular forms of expression.

Maria von Finckenstein, the respected Curator of Inuit Art at the Canadian Museum of Civilization, wrote about 'Becoming an Artist' in a remote Inuit community.

"Thomas Sivuraq, who now lives in Baker Lake, grew up a hunter in the Keewatin, the Barren Grounds, on the windswept tundra, in caribou country. His ancestors had developed a technology that helped them to survive in one of the world's most hostile environments. As a small boy, he could not wait to be taken on his first hunting trip by his father. His father taught him how to harness the dogs, how to navigate a sled over dangerous and unpredictable terrain, how to build an igloo, and how to stalk the caribou. To be a hunter was the only possible way of life. His driving ambition was to be a good hunter who provided successfully for his family. Disaster struck.

The caribou herds on which his camp depended for food and clothing changed their migration path, leaving the people destitute, without resources. World market prices for fox trapping had plummeted, jeopardizing income. Like so many of their ancestors who depended on game, the Sivuraq camp was in danger of starving to death. Sivuraq's siblings were rescued by government helicopters, but Thomas preferred to stay behind because his dogs, which he prized, did not fit into the airplane.

As a trapper, he depended on his dogs for tending his traplines and for occasional trips to the Baker Lake trading post. When his parents died,

Sivuraq lived alone for a while until, as he put it, he was at his wits' end. In desperation he attempted to walk with his dogs to the trading post. On his way he was picked up by another hunter travelling by kayak along the river leading to Baker Lake.

People from various camps had put up their igloos in Baker Lake, where they had become dependent on government relief. Sivuraq watched people bringing in carvings to the Hudson's Bay trading post and leaving with tea, flour, or ammunition. He decided to do the same. Somehow procuring stone, a hatchet, and an old file, he set to work. Thus began his career as a distinguished artist.

Sivuraq applied to this new activity the same discipline he had developed as a hunter. Successful hunting requires precise knowledge of the animals, the weather, and the land. He knew every cliff, valley, lake, stream, and landmark in his former hunting territory. This visual memory-we might call it a photographic memory-enabled him to detect the slightest change in weather conditions, which could often be a matter of life and death. So imagine the skills an experienced hunter like Sivuraq brought to carving: manual dexterity, keen observation, an extraordinary visual memory, intense focus and, a strict work ethic acquired during years of struggle for physical survival." (*Celebrating Inuit Art*, 1948-1970, Key Porter Books, 1999)

The intense focus of the Inuit weaver.

The extraordinary visual memory of the stone carver.

The manual dexterity of the print-maker.

Inuksuit.

The Inuit have lived in Nunatsiaq (the beautiful land) for over 4000 years; indeed a great human achievement.

The land and the sea provided everything the Inuit needed. With the exception of blocks of snow, used for winter shelters and certain traps, almost everything placed on the landscape was made with movable, unworked stone. Some objects were built to endure forever; others were fashioned with great skill but meant to vanish without a trace. Inuit throughout the Arctic knew of the existence of places of power. These places are numerous and varied, and include inuksuit, the stone structures of varied shape and size erected by Inuit for many purposes. Some were placed to be visible from a great distance, others to be hidden from casual view. Some were to be seen against a snowy backdrop, others situated on shore to be viewed from the sea or the ice.

Inuksuit vary not only in size and shape but also in their functions. One was to drive herds of game to where they would be killed in numbers. Another was to guide the hunter travelling on land, or on the sea or ice within sight of land. There are places in the Arctic where networks of inuksuit reach from the interior to the sea, and along the coast in both directions. (Canadian Museum of Civilization – Places of Power website.)

Canada's Peace Keepers

Of all the powers on the world stage, Canada is fortunate to belong to more multilateral clubs than almost any other nation on earth. Canadians are known to be proficient mediators and dedicated keepers and makers of international peace.

Some of the reasons for this internationalist instinct can be found in the accidents of history and geography. Former Prime Minister Pierre Trudeau once referred to one of the most important, when he said the fact that Canada 'sleeps with the elephant' means that we feel each 'twitch and grunt' of our great neighbour to the south, the United States of America.

Lester Pearson spent long years in the corridors of international diplomacy before becoming Prime Minister of Canada in 1963. He was part of a generation of idealistic, yet pragmatic post war multilateralists

Lester B. Pearson and Maryon, 1965.

who understood that peace was a long journey and that there were no shortcuts to freedom.

Present at the founding of the United Nations in 1945, this experienced Canadian diplomat would go on to become a trusted and respected voice in the international community. After winning the Nobel Peace Prize in 1957 for his invention of peace-

keeping at the time of the 1956 Suez crisis, the Pearson name would become synonomous with the work of generations of the blue berets in countries around the world.

Canadian peacekeepers served in Cyprus and Sarajevo; in Suez, Haiti, the Golan Heights, Namibia, Yugoslavia, Bosnia and East Timor. In fact, Canadians participated on nearly every peacekeeping mission established by the United Nations.

But whatever roads they travelled, the blue berets were to become symbols of hope in countries where hope had been forgotten. Their very presence brought solace to the victims of terror and ethnic conflict. Today, the Lester B. Pearson Peacekeeping Institute in Cornwallis, Nova Scotia trains peacekeepers and peacemakers from countries all around the world.

Canada's War Veterans

The poppy was adopted as the Flower of Remembrance for the war dead of Canada, Britain and a number of Commonwealth Countries.

IN FLANDERS FIELDS

In Flanders fields the poppies blow
Between the crosses, row on row,
That mark our place; and in the sky
The larks, still bravely singing, fly
Scarce heard among the guns below.

We are the Dead. Short days ago
We lived, felt dawn, saw sunset glow,
Loved, and were loved, and now we lie
In Flanders fields.

Take up our quarrel with the foe:
To you from failing hands we throw
The torch; be yours to hold it high.
If ye break faith with us who die
We shall not sleep, though poppies grow
In Flanders fields.

French translation

Au champ d'honneur, les coquelicots
Sont parsemé de lot en lot
Auprès des croix; et dans é'espace
Les alouettes devenues lasses
Mêlent leurs chants au sifflement
Des obusiers.

Nous sommes morts
Nous qui songions la veille encor'
À nos parents, à nos amis
C'est nous qui reposons ici,
Au champ d'honneur

À vous jeunes désabusés
À vous se porter l'oriflamme
Et de garder au fond de l'âme
Le goût de vivre en liberté.
Acceptez le défi, sinon
Les coquelicots se faneront
Au champ d'honneur.

French Translation (adaptation de Jean Pariseau, major du poème "In Flanders Fields" de John McCrae)

SUPPORTING ORGANISATIONS

United Nations Environment Programme (UNEP)

International Telecommunication Union (ITU)

An Initiative of information and communications technology service providers and suppliers, with the support of the United Nations Environment Programme and the International Telecommunication Union

Mission

To deliver our vision through:

¥ Sharing our experience and knowledge

¥ Working with our stakeholders

¥ Managing our operations in a sustainable way

¥ Raising awareness of the contribution that information and communications technology can make to society

¥ Research and benchmarking

To join **GeSI** or for more information, contact the **GeSI** Secretariat

UNEP Division of Technology, Industry and Economics

39-43 quai Andr Citro n, 75739 Paris Cedex 15 FRANCE

Tel: +33.1.44.37.14.50 ¥ Fax: +33.1.44.37.14.74 ¥ E-mail: gesi@unep.fr ¥ Web: www.gesi.org

Global e-Sustainability Initiative

Vision

Through the GeSI, we the information and communications technology industry aim to help improve the global environment and to enhance human and economic develop-ment, and thereby make a key contribution to a global sustainable future.

Initiative

The GeSI has been created by a number of major companies wishing to take a pro-active position on the impact their industry has on the environment and the contribution it can make to sustainable development globally. In particular we note the value of sharing learning across continents.

Our Objectives

As a collective voice, the members of the GeSI will help to influence policies of govern-ment, inform the public of its voluntary role in lowering the impact of development, and enjoy the rewards of promoting technology that fosters sustainable development.

Our Commitment

All signatory companies demonstrate a certain level of environmental achievement through entry criteria. We welcome both service operators and suppliers to help us to promote the information and communi-cations technology industry as socially responsible and progressive.

NOTES

The following is a summary of some of the principal sources used for this book.

Statistics Canada proved to be an invaluable and generous source of material. Statistics Canada information is used with the permission of the Minister responsible for Statistics Canada. Information on the availability of the wide range of data from Statistics Canada can be obtained from Statistics Canada's Regional Offices, its World Wide Web Site at http//www.statcan.ca, and its toll-free access number 1-800-263-1136.

The Canada Year Book, 1999 (Minister of Industry, Government of Canada, 1998), Catalogue No. 11-402-XPE, and *Canada: A Portrait* (Minister of Industry, Government of Canada, 1999) were used as reference sources. Material for the book was adapted from *Canada: A Portrait*, pps 6, 7, 41, 42, 51. As to the *Canada Year Book, 1999*, material was adapted from pps. 34-43. Material directly cited from p. 51.

Symbols of Canada (Canadian Heritage, Public Works and Government Services, Canada, 1999) was another excellent reference book. Background material on the provinces and the territories of Canada was adapted from pps. 20, 22, 24, 26, 28, 30, 32, 34, 36, 38, 40, 42, 44.

The list of background sources remains too lengthy to review, but some, particularly Craig Brown, ed. *The Illustrated History of Canada* (Key Porter Books, 1997) provide solid historical essays on Canada by some of the country's finest historians. Don Gilmour and Pierre Turgeon's beautifully written Canada, *A People's History*, Vol 1 (McClelland & Stewart, Canadian Broadcasting Corpor-

ation, 2000) is a fine source which is rich in illustrations and archival materials. Olive Patricia Dickason's *Canada's First Nations* (Oxford University Press, 1992) remains the most definitive on First Nations history in Canada. Peter McFarland and Wayne Haimila's *Ancient Land, Ancient Sky* (Alfred A. Knopf, 1999) is a rare and informative personalized account of Canada's First Nations. Maria von Finckenstein, ed. *Celebrating Inuit Art*, 1948–1970 (Canadian Museum of Civilization, Key Porter Books, 1999) contains a wonderful collection of essays featuring Maria von Finkenstein herself, along with the renowned James Houston, Ann Meekitjuk Hanson, and others. Peter C. Newman's invaluable work is widely known in Canada, but his essay entitled *'The Land That Shapes Us'* in Canada/ The Land That Shapes Us, Photography by Malak (Key Porter Books, 1997) is a masterful, instructive, yet moving look at the influence of Canada's geography on the development of the nation.

Two important Canadian journals were often consulted and reviewed as background sources, or for direct information cited within the text. *The Beaver: Canada's History Magazine*, founded in 1920 by the Hudson's Bay Company and published bimonthly by Canada's National History Society provides a fascinating look at the many faces of our history. *Canadian Geographic*, published by Canadian Geographic Enterprises on behalf of the Royal Canadian Geographic Society has been an instructive source of information for the book and is directly cited in several sections.

Carol Canada

Editor: Elizabeth McIninch
Photo Editor: Malak Karsh, O.C.
Design: Malak and Barbara Karsh,
    Elizabeth McIninch,
    Margo Smith
Cover Design: G.S.P. Communications

Film Work and Printing:
Main Cheong Paper Product Ltd.

ISBN O-9730179-0-2

ACKNOWLEDGEMENTS

Because of the scope of the Canada book in the New Millenium Series, the editor can only acknowledge the generous and efficient cooperation of a number of wonderful people who helped by contributing their expertise in a host of ways. Mrs. Barbara Karsh (Mrs. Malak) has been a constant source of professionalism, guidance and creativity. Senator Al Graham remained a great source of support in the development of the book, reviewing the copy, and remaining a continuing source of encouragement.

The unflappable Mr. Bruce Lloyd at St. Joseph's M.O.M. Printing, along with Elizabeth Payne and Margo Smith, brought their imagination, flair, and mastery of technology into the intricate task of developing the layout.

Many people generously offered their time in personal interviews and professional contributions which greatly enhanced the final work. The primary contributors and photographers are referred to throughout the volume. To all these fine Canadians, along with the wonderful photographers listed in the photo credits, I owe a deep debt of gratitude.

I have been privileged to have been able to speak with, and or work with, and learn from Mr. Ed Aquilina at Mayor Chiarelli's office, Ms. Suzanne Bergevin at Park's Canada, Dr. Wally Cherwinski at the National Research Council, Ms. Susan Fleck at Minister Handley's office in the Northwest Territories, Ms. Georgette Gaulin at Statistics Canada, Ms. Lisa Gregoire at the Edmonton Journal, Mr. Eric Harris at the Canadian Geographic, Mr. James Houston, world renowned authority on Inuit art and society, Ms. Pamela Leblanc at Industry Canada, Mr. Jeff Mahoney at Air Nunavut, Mr. Robert Peck at CAE, Mr. Robert Pichette on New Brunswick, Mr. Ralph Reschke at Alcan, Mr. Pierre Tanguay at Canam Steel, Mike Taylor and Anna Kapiniari at the Canadian Space Agency, Ms. Tracy Thiessen at Natural Resources, Mr. Harry Turner at the National Research Council, Maria von Finckenstein at the Museum of Civilization, Professor John Warkentin, noted Canadian geographer, Mr. Jonathan Wise at the Museum of Nature, Ms. Jonina Wood at Statistics Canada, and many others who volunteered their time and expertise in the interests of this project.

I would also like to thank some of the many people who offered information and photographs for the book, along with valuable suggestions. Space limitations prevent me from naming all those who helped. Mr. Don Baldwin at the Royal Canadian Legion, Mr. Emile Beauchamp at Industry Canada, Alexander Beggs at Innovation Place, Mr. Grosvenor Blair (descendent of Alexander Graham Bell), Annette Bourgeois at the Premier's office in Nunavut, Jennifer Bugden at Natural Resources, Doug Caldwell at the Premier's office in the Yukon Territory, Mary Kirby at National Defence, Diane Cunningham at Trojan Technologies.

Others included Julie Durand at Innu-Science, Patricia Dietz at Stora-Enso, Ms. Virginia Flood at the Lieutenant-governor's office in Prince Edward Island, Scoop Fredstrom at McCain's, Gilles Guitard at CAE, Ginette Gelinas at Canam Steel, Patrick Grenier at WECO, Ms. Debbie Harris at Ballard Technologies, Maureen A. Hope at the Lieutenant Governor's office in Nova Scotia, Mr. Ken Hovey at CTC Images, Jacques Larouche at Mayor Chiarelli's office, Josephine Laquian, Diane Mann at the Canadian Centre for Remote Sensing, Ms. Donna Manuel at Aquabounty, Sylvie Monette-Houle at GNA Alutech, Peter O'Brien's help at CPR, Marcie Stanley at Enterprise Cape Breton, Mary Ann Stewart at Palliser, Ms. Jocelyn Streimer, at Dr. Rey Pagtakhan's office, Linda Tardif, Pratt & Whitney, Kathryn Warden, Canada Light Source, Irene White at the office of the Lieutenant Governor of Saskatchewan, Alan Wojcik, Ontario Heritage Foundation, Mary Vincent, contributor to Canadian Geographic, and Carla Yuill at Nexen.

My deepest thanks to all!

Elizabeth

Photo Credits

Royal Canadian Mounted Police Charge.

The Maple Leaf

The maple leaf was historically used from the early days of Canada to symbolize the land and its people. It was first proposed as an emblem of Canada in 1834 when the Société Sainte-Jean-Baptiste was founded; shortly thereafter, in 1836, Le Canadien, a newspaper published in Lower Canada (now Québec), referred to it as a suitable emblem for Canada.

It was also used in the decorations for the visit of the Prince of Wales to Canada in 1860. It appears on the coats of arms granted to Québec and Ontario in 1868 and as a distinctive emblem on the royal arms of Canada proclaimed in 1921. The maple leaf was for many years the symbol of the Canadian Armed Forces and was used to identify the Canadian contingents in the two world wars. But it wasn't to receive official status until the National Flag of Canada was proclaimed by Her Majesty the Queen in 1965. (Canadian Heritage)